MW01241317

Culture Creators
Creating Culture for Your
Team or Organization

Willie Spears

"Coaching is a great way to impact young men, and those who take on the challenge carry huge responsibilities.

On the popular game show *Family Feud*, contestants were asked, "What is a profession that has great influence but is not respected?" The No. 1 answer was a teacher.

Willie Spears has been a great educator of young men on and off the field, and his worth to schools has gone unnoticed by many. As a nationally-renowned motivational speaker, his influence goes beyond his community and into the entire nation. His book *Culture Creators* contains the DNA for what it takes to build a culture the right way. His relationship with the Lord is evident in the way he lives his life and the culture he has created in his home, football teams, church, communities and schools.

Spears' nuggets of wisdom on building a culture that will last has been established by his successes in reaching young men and changing their attitudes for life."

~ Charlie Ward
Heisman Trophy Winner
NCAA Football National Champion
11-year NBA Veteran (Knicks, Spurs, Rockets)

To Tayelor and Kenneth,

I pray you realize the life you enjoy is the manifestation of the culture your mom has created for our home.

Praise for Culture Creators

"I have been around coaches and coaching for 40 years. I am constantly looking for ways to improve our program. This book by Willie Spears will help us win. Coach Spears has a great approach to coaching, especially the way that he deals with people. He tells some great stories, but more importantly, he gives hundreds of ideas that we can use in practical ways. Philosophy is one thing, but usable methods and systems separate the good from the great. That is what is so special about this book. The methods and systems that he describes can help anyone in any type of organization get better."

~ Rick Jones
8 Time State Champion, 5 State Runner-up
Hall of Fame, 16 time coach of the year
Head football coach
Greenwood High School
Greenwood, Arkansas

"As center director and Director of Education for Sylvan Learning Center for seven years, working in private and public schools for 11 years each, including seven years as a public school administrator, I have several tools that help me do my job effectively. *Culture Creators* is my new shiny tool. I recommend this resource to all school administrators. It is an easy read full of nuggets, strategies, stories and real-life solutions to common challenges in education."

~ Esi Shannon
Assistant Principal
Pensacola, Florida

"Any coach that has recruited Willie's school will tell you that the culture he has created is different from most places. His insight into how great teams are built sure does resonate with me because truly great teams don't come together out of chance. If you want to build a great organization, you have your starting point in Willie's book."

~ Tim Albin
Offensive Coordinator Ohio University
25-year college coach

"The two most important attributes of any school are strong instruction and culture. Mr. Spears has shared his proven methods of creating culture. We have used his materials in the past, and I am excited about sharing this resource with our faculty and staff."

~ Anthony Brock
Head of School
Valiant Cross Academy
Montgomery, Alabama

"In today's extremely competitive world, rather it be in business or sports, every organization has very talented people. However, the organization that has the right culture in place will be the most successful. Coach Spears lays out the perfect game plan in this book for any sports team or business organization looking to develop that right and winning culture to take their organization to that ultimate level of success."

~ Derrick Lett
Assistant Head Coach/Running Back Coach, Yale University

"Reading this book would be a valuable investment for any leader. CULTURE CREATORS is a crash course in creating culture, and it is packed with fresh, practical tips that can be implemented immediately."

~ Chanda Rigby
Head Women's Basketball Coach
Troy University

"The last 18 college games Willie played in were victories. I believe he took that winning culture and combined it with what he has learned in South Georgia, Alabama and Florida to create a winning formula. This book is really good. I hear his voice as I read the words. He has given us what he has learned from so many successful coaches and programs."

~ Brandon Hargers
Running Backs Coach
Carthage (Texas) High School
2013, 2016, 2017 State Champions

"Teaching and coaching for over 25 years in the public school, and now serving with the Fellowship of Christian Athletes the last two years, I can see Coach Willie Spears is right on in his assessment of changing the culture!"

~ Stacey Stewart
Director of Coaches Ministry
Southwest Florida Fellowship of Christian Athletes

"You must read Coach Willie Spears' proven ideas that can change a culture that produces mediocrity to one that produces maximum achievement. His practical approach applies to athletics, business, church and all organizations. I warn you – if you pay the price to apply his principles, you will be a different leader! You will also become a culture changer!"

~ Dr. John Ed Mathison
36-year Senior Minister
Frazer Memorial United Methodist
johnedmathison.org

For the past five years I have communicated with 20 leaders a year and asked each of them 20 questions. As a coach, I have talked to coaches of different sports on various levels. As an evangelist, I have spoken with ordained ministers from many denominations. As a small business owner, I have spoken with successful small business owners from different parts of the country. As an entertainer, I have studied successful entertainers. What I have found from these different walks of life is several common denominators. No matter the profession, each leader is a dedicated hard worker who persevered through failure and defeat; but what stood out among them all was their attention to detail in shaping the culture of their team, audience, customers, or employees.

One of my friends called me one day in preparation for an interview as an assistant coach with the Seattle Seahawks. He asked me to give him a quick "pep talk" before his initial interview. I provided the pep talk. Weeks later, when my friend got the job, he shared with me his interview experience. My friend said that only five or six teams have a legitimate chance of winning the Super Bowl and Seattle is one of them.

"Why?" I asked.

"The Seattle Seahawks' culture shapes their decisions." My friend went on to explain that every team has talent, money, facilities and a fan base; however, most teams don't know how to implement a winning culture.

In 2000, I sat in a Renaissance Hotel conference room in Orlando, Florida, with several other prospective employees for a training with Disney Cruise Line. I was applying for a position as an entertainer on one of their new cruise ships. For two days, we sat through what I now realize was culture training. The Walt Disney Company is one of the most successful companies in the world with a market cap of $150 billion. My two years with Disney taught me the importance of culture and climate. Their secrets to success have shaped my way of thinking.

When I made the decision to go into education and later coaching, I sat down with top principals and coaches to ask them to what do they contribute their success. The overwhelming response was culture. After spending time under the top high school football coach in Georgia, a Hall of Fame coach in Florida and a top high school football coach in the state of Arkansas, I realized my methodology on culture was spot on.

This book is a recipe for success. Inside it are the ingredients for improving your team, business, school, or organization. I have taken what I have learned and experienced and placed it into your hands. I have served as head football coach of six high schools not because I'm a good coach, but because our cultural mindset has a positive effect on schools and communities. I was selected as the first African-American head coach three times and athletic director once because of data-driven results related to culture. I have been a part of a national championship, state championship, and several conference championships and have made history more than 20 times by implementing qualitative methods through practical application. Every school where we have served felt the difference when we left if they didn't cultivate what we started. You can see it in the amount of referrals, you can hear it from the student body, and you can feel it in the air and see it in the program. What we do is not magical, but practical. Not unprecedented, just unpracticed.

What strength and conditioning did for high school sports 20 years ago, creating culture is doing today. What technology has done for the Corporate America and the music industry, culture is doing now. Coaches, do you remember how Hudl changed the way we do things? Creating a positive culture is that. Creating culture is the new paradigm shift. Screaming at kids and cussing them out doesn't work anymore. Leading out of fear is the old way of doing things. Culture Creators is to leaders what the Apple phone was to consumers back in January 2009. It's new, evolving, important, and ever-changing.

Google, Apple, Walmart, Exxon Mobil, Berkshire Hathaway and McKesson are among the top companies in the country. They all have impeccable customer service relating to culture; however, they had to make major changes on their way to reaching the top. Everyone wants to be at the top, but no one wants to climb.

If you are willing to get outside your comfort zone and embrace change through creating culture, I believe your team, business, or organization will win with people, not just with numbers.

Chapter 1
Cultural Thermostat

We are all responsible for the culture of our group. In this book I use examples from my life as a coach to teach about the importance of culture. However, anyone can relate to and use these strategies in their business, organization, company, church, team, school or family. Culture and leadership are synonymous. Therefore, even if you don't have the title of president, manager or leader, you still are a leader. In order to change culture we must think like an owner not an employee, a leader not a follower. Everyone has to answer to someone, but everyone also is leading someone. Our first leadership roles often start with our families.

My family and I love ice cream and milkshakes. I'm a Cold Stone Neapolitan guy. My daughter loves Hershey's Superman ice cream. My wife and son don't have a favorite, but they never turn down an opportunity to go with Tayelor and I. One day after church we went to Bruster's because there isn't a Cold Stone or Hershey's in Montgomery, Alabama, where we live. The group in front of us ordered five milkshakes. The young lady working behind the counter told them she was very sorry because the milkshake machine was broken. After that family left, the young lady asked our family what we wanted to order. I told her I had wanted a milkshake but now needed to look at the menu and decide what else I wanted because I knew the milkshake machine was broken. The young lady corrected me and said the milkshake machine was not broken. I gave her a strange look, to which she replied, "I didn't feel like making five milkshakes, so I told that family it was broken

Leadership is Ownership

She was thinking like an employee, not an owner. Her goal was to get a paycheck, not to add value to the company or customer. A person with an owner mentality would not turn down an opportunity to grow the business in every way. An employee mentality is one that lacks initiative. An owner mentality says, "I have to make things better, because I own this." As athletic director, I would tell our head coaches to spend the school's money like it was theirs, not like it belonged to the school. We are all owners, leaders, presidents, CEOs, principals, and head coaches.

University of West Florida Head Football Coach Pete Shinnick does not allow profanity to infiltrate the culture of the Argonauts. He is able to instill this form of discipline because he is the head football coach. However, when he was the tight end coach at another university, he could not request this form of discipline from the entire team. Although he was not the head coach of the team, he realized he was the head coach of the tight ends. His tight ends were not allowed to use profanity. He was later promoted to offensive line coach, then offensive coordinator. With each promotion he made a conscious decision to create a disciplined culture within his groups.

We all are in charge of a large or small segment of society. Decide what is important to you. Have a plan. Cast your vision, make it stick, and be consistent. This book will help you create your desired culture on and off the field, in and out of the office, on or off the court. You will learn how to develop your team, serve your customers, build your brand, market your products and become a high performer.

Andy Stanley is the pastor of North Point Community Church in Alpharetta, Georgia. When it comes to building a church he is one of the highest performers. According to msn.com, his church is the second largest church in the United States. While preaching one Sunday, Pastor Stanley, who goes by Andy, noticed world-renowned leadership expert John Maxwell sitting in the front row taking notes. Andy said to himself, "What am I going to say that John Maxwell needs to write down?"

The Renaissance Hotel, in downtown Montgomery, Alabama, used to host an annual coaching clinic that featured top high school and college coaches. One year, there was a high school coach from a small town talking about the proper way to execute a football play known as "the power." While this little-known, modestly-paid teacher with the title of head coach explained how to pull, kick, wrap, and log, Auburn University Head Football Coach Gus Malzahn sat in the front row and took notes.

I once heard someone say when referring to an owner, "If I had their money I wouldn't work." I did not respond, but in my head I thought, "That's why you don't have their money." John Maxwell and Gus Malzahn are game-changers in their professions, and they both have decided they must continue learning. Are you a game-changer or a sandwich-eater? A game-changer is intentional when it comes to making a difference. A sandwich-eater is only concerned with what they can get from the team or organization. I had a player who ate pre- and post-game meals, with no intention of getting in the game. He was a sandwich-eater, not a game-changer.

> **A short pencil is better than a long memory**

As the leader in the room, your group will take on your personality while in the workplace. Do you look at your phone, constantly checking the time, or are you a person who stays late? Are you the first to arrive and start the first pot of coffee and the last one to leave, cleaning the pot for the next day? Or do your hobbies, apps, friends, and social media get more of your attention? Do you have on a bib or an apron? Are

> **Do you have on a bib or an apron?**

> **What you do speaks so loudly that I can barely hear what you say**

you here to serve or be served? Everything rises and falls on leadership. Your room, team, or group will meet the bar you set for them with your actions. What you do speaks so loudly that people can barely hear what you say. It is the job of the one creating the culture to change the temperature of the room.

When it comes to culture and climate, are you a thermostat or a thermometer? In order to get the most out of this resource you will need to spend time looking in the mirror. Self-evaluation, self-assessment, and self-reflection are keys to consistent growth. We all have the ability to improve. However, we may not have the resolve. Is it the goal of your team, church, organization, or business to survive or to thrive? In her book *Daring Greatly*, Dr. Brené Brown used a quote from U.S. President Theodore Roosevelt as her thesis to highlight the advantages of vulnerability. Vulnerability is uncomfortable, just like sitting in a room with the wrong temperature. Are you a thermometer or a thermostat?

A thermometer reflects the temperature of the culture or environment. It simply reacts to what is already happening. If the temperature is cold, it tells you exactly that. If it is hot, the thermometer reflects that reality as well. It is an unintelligent instrument. It is limited. It is the opposite of a smartphone. Smartphones have several functions while the thermometer has one.

However, a thermostat regulates the culture or environment. Compared with the thermometer, a thermostat is artificial intelligence. It sets the desired temperature of the room, and more than that, the thermostat signals the air conditioner to crank up and cool the room down. If the temperature falls below the desired temperature, the thermostat causes the heater to turn on in order for the room to warm up. This instrument has multiple functions with one goal of keeping the room a constant temperature. The thermostat is intelligent in the sense that it consistently monitors the environment, and if the temperature gets too hot or cold, the thermostat decides what to do to correct the situation.

Are you consistently monitoring your culture, making the correct adjustments to maintain the desired culture? Thermostat leaders have a pulse on the morale, efficiency, stress level, and cultural conditions of their organization. When the temperature gets hot due to a lack of resources, having more work than there is time, or unrealistic deadlines that cause stress, thermostat leaders cool things off by acting as the calming influence with the organization. They take time to listen to the concerns of their team members and provide the necessary direction and support that is needed to help the team achieve its goals. Thermostat leaders alleviate pressure on their team by mixing in fun activities, impromptu snacks, videos, and communication.

In the same way, during the off season or downtime when work is slow, thermostat leaders get their teams focused on the vision, purpose, and goals of the team. Because they are actively monitoring the culture of their organization, they know when the team needs tough love or when it is time to set new goals.

Thermostat leaders build trust and confidence with their team members, while thermometer leaders cause trust to evaporate. Trust is vital if your organization is going to experience consistent success. Employees who feel trusted by their leaders have greater confidence in their work. They put in extra effort, and they are more productive in their roles. When teammates trust the leader, they learn to trust each other. They stay in their lanes and do their jobs.

On the other hand, employees who do not feel trusted put in less effort, are less productive, and will find a way to quit because they aren't emotionally invested.

Here are five ways a leader can build trust within a team:

1. Encourage your team members to take risks.
2. Show confidence in your team; don't micromanage.
3. Show members that you care about them outside the workplace.
4. Give them influence over the things that affect them the most.
5. Publicly show support for the work they do.

> **When you know your worth you will stop giving discounts**

It is important to realize that you and your organization are worth the best. When you know your worth, you will stop giving discounts. Don't lower the bar. Maintain a culture of excellence.

One of my closest friends harps on the importance of excellence all the time. Donte Sheppard worked with me in Pensacola and for a short time in Vernon before leaving to take a Division One coaching job in Kentucky. He says: What gets seen gets acknowledge, what gets acknowledged gets respected, what gets respected gets done and what gets done gets adopted.

Maintain a culture of excellence and your staff and players will adopt your behaviors.

Chapter 2
What is Culture?

Your organization probably has some sort of measuring system to identify effectiveness. We use a table to measure culture. This table consists of five columns and up to 15 organizational systems. I will share the first organizational system with you. We share the other 14 systems during our presentations on creating culture.

Culture Rubric:

Organizational System: Leader Tone

Advanced:
- Leaders are always upbeat, motivational, and inspiring.
- Positive framing: leaders narrate the positive student behaviors (rather than calling out the negative) and use praise, challenge, and aspiration to motivate the team member.
- Leaders are attentive to every detail in practice and address those that are out of place immediately.
- Leaders carry themselves with confidence and authority so that organization members are keenly aware of their presence.

Proficient:
- Leaders are most often upbeat, motivational, and inspiring with occasional moments of ineffective tone,

7

language or delivery.
- Positive framing: leaders almost always narrate the positive team member behaviors (only rarely calling out the negative) and use praise, challenge and aspiration to motivate the student athletes
- Leaders are attentive to most details in practice and address those that are out of place quickly.
- Leaders carry themselves with confidence and authority so that organization members are aware of their presence.

Working Towards:
- Leaders seem overwhelmed or aloof and only make occasional attempts at being motivated and inspiring.
- Leaders narrate negative rather than positive conduct.
- Leaders are inconsistent with recognizing details and/or addressing them quickly.
- Acts of organization member misconduct occur within the presence of the leader.

Needs Improvement:
- Leaders seem overwhelmed, aloof, and do not make occasional attempts at being motivated and inspiring.
- Leaders are mostly negative in their interactions with members of the organization.
- Leaders do not recognize details and/or do not address them quickly.
- Acts of misconduct occur within the presence of the leader.

This rubric, or checklist, should guide you on your journey to creating a desired culture conducive to growth and learning. These principles work for all organizations, including schools, teams, churches, businesses, and corporations. Looking back on my adolescent years, I can see where my team fell short according to the rubric. This evaluation helps me improve as a leader today.

In 1991, I was a skinny middle school football player

in Panama City, Florida. I played for Coach Kent and Coach Harrell at Rosenwald Middle School. At the time we had three high schools in our city. Now, Panama City has twice as many high schools that sponsor football teams. Back then, none of us thought about going to a school that was not in our zone or close to our home. I was an only child, and no one in my family played football, but my youth league coach had a son named Jermaine who played for Mosley High School. My father never went to high school, and my mother went to Bay High School. However, I was zoned for Rutherford High School, which had just come off a 22-game losing streak.

Although I went on to become an above-average high school football player, played on a team in college that won a national championship, and then played indoor professional football, I was unaware of these possibilities in 1991. Back then I did not know one person who played college football, and I had never seen a college football game live or on television. My parents weren't into sports or television. However, they were into me and were amazing supporters. Up until that point, I had played football and baseball for six years but had no dreams of playing sports in college. I did not own a Florida State University or Florida Gator tee-shirt. I did, however, like to make fun of all my teachers who were FSU graduates when Miami won because of a missed field goal, or extra point, now famously known as "Wide Right."

Of the three kickers who missed game-changing field goals in the Florida State vs. Miami rivalry, two of them were coached by my high school football coach. Dan Mowrey played for Coach Steve Hardin at Lincoln High School in Tallahassee, Florida, before going on to Florida State. Matt Munyon played for Coach Hardin at Rutherford High School in Panama City, Florida, as an exceptional receiver and kicker before joining the Seminoles in Tallahassee. Those missed attempts helped create culture in the Sunshine State. Coach Hardin changed the culture of Rutherford High School in the '90s, and this had a tremendous impact on the entire state.

In his first interview with local sports anchor Scott Rossman, Coach Hardin said, "It's not when we're going to win. It's how many we're going to win." WHAT?!? Coach Steve Hardin came to Rutherford in 1991 from Lincoln High School and overnight completely changed the culture of the entire city. He took over a team that was one loss away from tying the state record for 22 consecutive losses. That fall, after losing to Port Saint Joe High School in the season opener, Rutherford tied the record. What happened next is nothing short of amazing.

During the next 10 years, Coach Hardin's team averaged 10 wins a season, played for two state championships, received national recognition in high school polls, had more student-athletes go on to play college football than anyone in the city, and raised the level of play for every school in the area.

In 1993, the three schools in the city were among the best in the state of Florida. Rutherford and Bay competed against each other in the semi-finals for the second largest classification in the state but lost in the regular season to crosstown rival Mosley High School, which played in the largest classification in the state. The semi-final game was televised, and extra bleachers were brought in to hold the crowd of close to 20,000. Although Rutherford defeated Bay in the regular season to claim the conference championship, Bay played an exceptional game in the rematch. This was only the second season where the conference runner-up was allowed to compete in the playoffs. In years past only the conference champion was allowed to compete for a state championship. Bay defeated Rutherford 38-0 on its way to losing the state championship game to Bradenton Southeast.

This all happened because Steve Hardin changed the culture of football in Bay County. He created a fictitious coaching rivalry between himself and Bay High Coach Jim Scroggins. He once told me that it is the job of the head football coach to sell tickets. One way he accomplished this was by creating a culture where the public thought he detested the head coach from the rival school. The community thought he could not stand Coach Scroggins. The truth was, he respected Coach Scroggins and thought a lot of him. He understood that perception was reality. The goal was to fill the stands, sell tickets, concessions, and make the game relevant.

Only wear school colors

Coach Hardin would not allow us players to wear the colors of any other team when we were working out or at practice. We could wear neutral colors: black, white, or grey - or our school colors. Those were our choices. Coach Hardin thought outside the box in the early '90s. He worked it out that the youth league teams on our side of town used our *term-aknowledgy* and ran our system. He hired the youth league coaches and the middle school coach. This was unheard of. He also started a youth league camp. I have met grown men who rave about the camp and how they attended from age 6 through high school.

Coach Hardin also called maintenance about filling potholes in the school parking lot and painting dirty stucco above the lunchroom. The beautification of the school was important because he expected a record number of college recruiters to show up to recruit his players. He participated in local advertising campaigns, coached youth baseball, and scheduled schools from several different states.

By playing teams from other states he created a culture of superiority. This also gave the team national exposure. In a world before social media and smartphones, newspapers and magazines had all the power. Prep Sports writers were important. Coach Hardin had writers in several states writing about Springfield Rutherford. I met a high school coach from Minnesota who talked about Springfield Rutherford as if Springfield was a metropolis - rather than a suburb of Panama City with a population of less than 10,000 citizens. By playing teams in other states, Coach Hardin created a culture of prominence.

We had no idea that the teams we were playing were evenly matched because he led us to believe they were the top teams in the state. These and other decisions changed

11

the culture of the school and the football program. Coach Hardin's impact was so undeniable that in 1992 he was named teacher of the year without having taught a single class.

Another way Coach Hardin changed the culture is through the way he raised funds and built the booster club. He implemented strategies on how to sell fundraiser cards. Everyone does this now, but he would drop players off - with their jerseys on - in neighborhoods and put several players in front of department stores, depending on each player's demeanor, attitude, and personality.

So, you might be asking, what exactly is culture? Culture is the culmination of characteristics that make up the environment in which you dwell.

A thriving high school culture produces student athletes that run on and off the field, clean the locker room, set the tone for acceptable behavior on campus, and treat people with respect. The examples I gave about Coach Hardin define culture.

If I see rat droppings in your locker room, office, or gymnasium, I don't have to see the rat. The droppings are evidence that you have a rodent. The same is true of culture. I can visit your organization for 20 minutes and tell you the climate of your organization. I speak to churches, teams, schools, and executives in corporate America often. I would say that more than 70 percent of the places I go have an undesirable culture. Climate and culture are a manifestation of the organization's leadership. The leader is either teaching the undesirable behavior or allowing it to happen.

Chapter 3
How Did We Get Here?

How long did it take for your organization to come to the place it finds itself when relating to culture? I have worked in some really bad school districts. One district was ranked the worst school district in the country, according to an article published in the Seattle Times. One high school in that district had 11 principals in 13 years. Another school district was taken over by the state, which concluded the district had failed to educate students and should lose its eligibility to continue educating students. The suggestion was made to take the districts' accreditation and replace the public school systems in place with charter schools.

Back to our original question: how long did it take for your current culture to get to where it is? I would imagine it didn't happen overnight, and it took time to arrive at its current location. If it took time to get to where we are, it will take time to get to where we want to go. Don't rush the process of creating culture. Like a good steak, it will take time.

Abraham Lincoln said if he had six hours to cut down a tree he would spend four hours sharpening his blade. You've heard of the four Ps? *Proper*

> **Abraham Lincoln said if he had six hours to cut down a tree he would spend four hours sharpening his blade.**

Preparation Prevents Poor Performance. If we fail to plan, we plan to fail. Do you have a plan for creating a thriving culture in your organization? Do you know the culture you want to have? There should be an emotional attachment to your desired culture. What does it feel like? What does it look like? What does it smell like?

When I walked in Willie Durham State Farm Agency in central Alabama I smelled the aroma of specialty coffee. A receptionist greeted me and asked if I would like coffee or water. Others in the clean office smiled and welcomed me as if I were someone special. I was hired to provide professional development for Willie Durham's staff that morning, and I figured they wanted to put their best foot forward before we started our session. However, this was not the case. This was not my first time in the office. During other visits I noticed his staff granting everyone this same treatment. It was part of their culture. Once you are in that sort of environment it gets all over you. If you entered a mining shaft the particles in the air would attach themselves to your person. This is unavoidable. Culture is inclusive. An unproductive culture will affect people, and they will not even realize it.

As a teenager, I worked in a restaurant, and I remember watching the adults with the strongest personalities change the culture of the restaurant crew every few months. This one guy helped several young people find confidence in smoking. Many of the teenagers there never smoked until they started hanging out with this guy. Some of them did smoke, but never in public, until his influence changed their culture. The same was true when it came to a number of other things, like partying, tattoos and the need for money. However, other people changed the culture in positive ways, including saying a blessing over food. There was an older gentleman who used to say grace, or a blessing over his food, every time he would eat with us. A few weeks later, we all started doing the same thing.

David Brumfield was on staff when I took over as head coach and athletic director in Jefferson County. We called him Coach B, and he said it best. He said, "Coach, these kids are followers. Last year, they were cussing and fussing every day, they got in fights with coaches, shouting matches, and they had no respect for the facility or for one another. This year they don't cuss each other out; they respect one another, and they treat the coaches different. They are just followers." His statement was evidence of a changing culture. He was an amazing man who taught me so much. He is one of two coaches I have had on my staff that have passed away. Words cannot describe how it feels to lose Coach B, as well as Gary Edwards from Live Oak, Florida.

Gary was the most beloved person in the community. He had the unique ability of bringing cultures together. He was a school resource officer and the head of the Police Athletic League. You could drive around Live Oak and ask any self-proclaimed redneck to list his best friends, and he would mention Gary Edwards in his top five. Take five minutes and introduce yourself to the self-proclaimed neighborhood thug, and you would hear Gary's name again. There were more than 2,000 people at his funeral. I assured the crowd that none of us would have that many people at our funerals because we don't have Coach Edwards' gift of creating culture. He made everyone feel important, and that's key.

The thriving culture of high school football recruiting in the south is unparalleled. I could tell you stories that would make this book an excellent research document for *ESPN Outside the Lines*. One of the more exciting parts of being a head high school football coach is meeting other coaches during the recruiting process. No sport recruits players the way high school football does. Most sports use the Amateur Athletic Union or AAU to find talent, whereas football still sends coaches to high schools to build relationships with the high school football coach in an effort to gain favor with the recruit.

It is always interesting to me to hear how coaches got to their current spots. For instance, Nick Saban started at his alma mater Kent State University as a graduate assistant in 1973. He went on to have stops at Syracuse, West Virginia, Ohio State, Navy, Michigan State, Houston Oilers, Toledo, Cleveland Browns, Michigan State again, LSU, Miami Dolphins and now Alabama. He coached for 17 years before becoming a head coach and for 27 years before winning a national championship.

Each coach's journey is interesting. I try to read a book a month, and the book I'm currently reading is called *COACH*. It's about a coach who got out of coaching to start selling insurance. He became a millionaire. It's an unbelievable story. The part to which many coaches can relate is the moving around from job to job for different reasons. Coach Art Williams from Cairo, Georgia, bounced around a little before building the greatest term life insurance company in the world. The same is true of Les Steckel. In his book *One Yard Short* he talks about waiting for the phone to ring and walks the reader through the hiring season for coaches. It's really good.

My coaching journey should have started two years before it did. I was blessed to play college ball for a man named Tim Albin, who is currently the offensive coordinator at Ohio University. He attended Northwestern Oklahoma State University in Alva, Oklahoma, and later became the head coach there. Although I had been featured in a *Forrest Davis Football Recruiting Annual* magazine, I wasn't as good as I thought I was. I was 5 feet, 9 inches tall and 155 pounds. I ran a 4.6 in the 40-yard dash. On top of that, my grade point average was 2.5, and I scored a 17 on the ACT! This meant those letters from universities like Baylor, Florida and Cincinnati didn't mean anything. What did mean something for sure, though, was that I had a coach who knew how to find schools for his players.

I ended up at Northwestern Oklahoma State University (NWOSU) with three junior college transfers from my same high school. Attending NWOSU turned out great for me. I was part of a 31-game winning streak, the first national championship for the university in any sport, and I graduated. The only part I missed out on was the opportunity to coach.

My first year at NWOSU I was ineligible. This meant I was able to take classes and practice, but I could not dress out and play in any games. Four years later I graduated, but I still had one more year of eligibility. Coach Albin had just taken a job as an assistant coach at the University of Nebraska and suggested to me that I should play one more season at NWOSU to work on my master's degree and start my coaching career. He told me the team needed my leadership more than my athletic ability and that this decision would help me down the road.

In spite of the fact that I was lucky enough to score the touchdown to seal our national championship, I was nowhere near the most athletic player on our team. We were NAIA (National Association of Intercollegiate Athletics), not NCAA (National Collegiate Athletic Association). We were not in the top class of college sports, but rather, we were in what is considered a lower class. With that being said, I believe we could have competed with the bottom half of the NCAA Division I schools. Many sports writers believed the same thing, ranking NWOSU the top NAIA program of all time. We had close to 20 players who made it onto an NFL roster during the four years I was there.

I should have listened to Coach Albin and started my coaching career with Coach Garin Higgins at NWOSU, but I didn't. I was homesick and wanted to go back to Florida. Plus, I thought I would not need a master's degree or coaching experience. Boy, was I wrong.

In 2001, I still had hopes and dreams of playing in the NFL. I was in the NFL Europe draft but never got a call. I had a tryout with the Canadian Football League, but I didn't run fast enough. I tried to stay in shape by playing with indoor professional leagues, such as the Arena Football League, while working as a substitute teacher at my old high school. After school, I would hang around and help out wherever the coaches would let me. One day my old wide receiver coach Mark Stanton pulled me to the side and asked me if I wanted to coach full time. I wasn't sure I wanted that, but I was sure that I wanted to hear what he had to say.

During the spring semester, Coach Stanton told me that he would not be there in the fall, but he couldn't tell Coach Hardin because his new job would not start until August. At the time, I really didn't understand the business very well, but I shook my head and said OK. He said if I wanted to be the next wide receiver coach at Rutherford High School, this was my opportunity. So I waited a few days and went in to talk to Coach Hardin about the possibility of one day coaching receivers. He assured me that the job would not come open for a while and that I needed to keep helping out where I could.

That summer, I was working out of town when my dad called me and said Coach Hardin had left a message for me. The message said that I had one day to come and talk to him about this wide receiver position. I have always been intimidated by my former head football coach. Therefore, I was in his office the next day. We talked, and he explained to me that if he put the job on the classified board, he would receive several applications. I did not realize it, but working at Rutherford High School in the 1990s and early 2000s was a really big deal.

Coach used to tell us that when we go to coaching clinics people would crowd around us and ask us how we do what we do. He would say in his high-pitched voice, "Willie, when they see that Ram on your collared shirt, they will ask you how we run the 'alley oop.'" The alley oop was our fade - or nine route. We ran it better than anyone in the state. That's not my opinion. That's what the stats say.

We were throwing the ball way before the spread offense took off. At one time, Coach Hardin's three sons were all listed in the top 10 of career passing leaders in the state. Come to find out, he wasn't exaggerating. During my first clinic several coaches asked me about our fade route.

My first football clinic was in Okaloosa Island in the panhandle of Florida. I remember it like it was yesterday. Andy McCollum was the head coach at Middle Tennessee; Larry Fedora was the passing game coordinator (a new title back then) at the University of Florida. The UF defensive back coach's name was Woody, and he had just won the lottery. Coach Fedora went over the keys to success as part of his presentation. One of the keys he mentioned was to practice how you play. He pointed out that Woody said they played press man, but when they got in the game against the University of Miami, they played at 10 yards and back-peddled before the snap of the ball. Woody came down the aisle from the back of the room, and it almost got physical. It was hilarious.

In 2003, I went to my first Fellowship of Christian Athletes leadership football camp in Black Mountain, North Carolina. The camp leader in charge of football was Mark Hudspeth. He was the head football coach at the University of North Alabama at the time. Out of 100-plus coaches in the room, he picked me to be over the receivers at the camp. I didn't feel I was experienced enough to lead receivers from more than 100 high schools. At the time, I did not realize the culture Coach Hardin created had prepared me for this moment. At this camp, I realized my way of coaching was rare and unique. That week I was offered several jobs. This changed the way I looked at coaching. I went back home with a new confidence and a dream to become a head coach one day.

After working at Rutherford for five years and coaching several sports, I left to take a head coaching position in track and girls basketball at Arnold High School on Panama City Beach. I felt I had paid my dues, and it was time for me to be a head coach in another sport to gain some head coaching experience. Although I got paid to coach football, I coached track and weightlifting for free while at Rutherford. I learned so much in those five years, but I had so much more to learn.

One of my pet peeves about young coaches is their lack of thirst for knowledge. I have worked on several different coaching staffs, and as a head coach and athletic director, I have hired several coaches. Eight of my former assistants have served as head football coaches and several others as head coaches of other sports. I love it when a coach has worked their way up, and they are coaches, not specialists.

I have met coaches who knew nothing about fundraising, the weightroom, equipment room, how to line a field, break down film, do laundry, talk to parents or check grades. I believe after five years of coaching in any sport you should know the basics of all things involved in coaching. It is the same with our players. In sports, we used to focus on fundamentals, but now we seem to give the ball to the best player and let them do what they want to do so they won't get mad and transfer.

I have been accused of attracting transfers. I was actually fired for recruiting. After the investigation, they said I was innocent, but as you will learn in a later chapter, culture recruits itself. When I went to Arnold, no players followed me, but people said they did. People also said that I and another coach contributed to the downfall of the Rutherford program. In this business you have to develop thick skin and keep a small circle. I have developed the skill of not always valuing other people's opinions. The only opinions I always value are those given by people in my small circle.

In 2009, I was voted Coach of the Year. A local sports writer wrote, "Give Willie Spears a hat and a whistle, and he will turn your program around." The same sports writer wrote in 2011, "Who hired Willie Spears? He has no idea what he's doing." I am not Nick Saban, Bill Belichick, Urban Meyer or Bobby Bowden, but every one of these men have had nasty things written about them. It comes with the profession.

I was really excited about sitting under Coach James Hale at Arnold High School. He had won several games down south and won more games in Panama City than anyone else during his time there. He was winning football games at the beach school. Not golf, tennis and swimming, but Arnold was the best football school in the city. His wife was the athletic director, and the principal, John Haley, was my old Sunday school superintendent. In this business it is important to network - go to the conventions and work camps - and build relationships. I have been offered several college opportunities just because of the contacts I have made.

I drove from Springfield to Panama City Beach in 2006 to do spring football with Arnold High School. The spring was good, and the summer was even better. Arnold had the best weightlifting program in the city. They went on to win two state championships in weightlifting. That summer I spent time doing my head coaching duties as the head girl's basketball coach and all my duties as an assistant football coach.

One day I got a call from Richie Marsh, who was the head football coach in Thomasville, Georgia. We had met a few years earlier when Rick Darlington was the head football coach at Valdosta High School in Valdosta, Georgia. Coach Marsh was one of his defensive coordinators. He said he had a position on his staff for me if I wanted it, but it was already the middle of July. I had to ask myself what I should do. Should I leave my hometown to move to Georgia? This was not the first good job offer I had received, but this one really had me thinking.

A year earlier I was offered a position on Bill Castle's staff as a wide receiver coach. That team was loaded with Division I athletes. They had nine players from the same high school team go on to play at the University of Florida.

I turned down the opportunity because my wife was pregnant, and we had another little baby who wasn't even a year old yet. This was the second great job opportunity I had been offered, and I didn't know what to do.

I found the Bible verse Proverbs 16:9. It says, "A man's heart plans his way, but the Lord directs his steps." I have used this verse to help me with all my career decisions.

As a play-caller, I knew before the game what we were going to call on fourth and short. We were going to call

> **A man's heart plans his way, but the Lord directs his steps.**

> **If you fail to plan, you plan to fail.**

"Bandit Right Victor Texas." As a head coach, I knew before the game what I would do at the end of the game - go for 2 to win or go for the tie. I determined this by where we were playing and who I thought had the better team. When it comes to making tough decisions in your career you must have a plan before situations arise.

I think it is important to have a decision-making process before you get in a situation where you will be forced to make a big decision. My decisions were based on my goals. One of my goals was to become a head football coach. I believe teaching is the greatest profession because teachers teach all professions. I thought that if I could be the one in charge, I could make decisions that would help players and coaches grow as people, not just as coaches and athletes. What are your decision-making principles? What are your goals? Are they about money? Status? Position? Upward mobility?

> **Teaching is the greatest profession because teachers teach all professions.**

Coach Marsh offered me and my wife jobs that would increase our combined salaries by $15,000. He offered me a co-offensive coordinator position and a chance to coach in famed South Georgia football. I took it. My wife and I took our two young children, who were 1 and 2 years old at the time, to Thomasville, Georgia.

I never asked what kind of offense he ran. I never asked what my wife's job would be. I never asked how much input would I have on the offense. I never asked what his expectations were of me. I never asked anything. Big mistake. However, it turned out great. Working for Coach Marsh changed my coaching philosophy.

Billy Graham said a coach will impact more lives

in one year than most people will in their entire lifetime. Coach Marsh embodied this statement. I call him Jesus Christ with a whistle. He was incredible. I was already a Christian, and I was already a coach, but he taught me how to be a Christian Coach, not just a coach that's a Christian. He was tough, hard-nosed, no-nonsense. Our personalities were completely opposite. He wanted to run inside veer and midline, while I wanted to throw hitch, slant and fade all day. In my mind, the three-step drop and high-percentage passing was the answer. In his mind, running the ball, controlling the game, playing great defense and special teams were the answer. Needless to say we had conflict.

How do you handle conflict? It is best to have a plan for that as well, and not wait until you are in a situation. Smart people think about the future. Coach Marsh may not want to admit this, but he really didn't need my offensive expertise on his staff. He was a white man who understood

A coach will impact more lives in one year than most people will an entire lifetime.

the value of having a black man with family values on his staff. The other offensive coordinator, Tim Price, and Coach Marsh knew way more than I did about football. I learned so much from those two. That year changed the way I coached.

Coaches often contact me during the off-season to ask my advice on becoming a head coach. The one thing I think you need to do is simply apply. I believe interview experience is important, and applying is the best way to get real interview

Smart people think about the future.

experience. Later in the book, I give you my tricks to land an interview. During that off-season in Thomasville I applied for the head coaching position at Chiles High School in nearby Tallahassee, Florida. I am sure I wasn't the most qualified, but somehow I got an interview.

This was my first interview for a head football coaching position. Since that time, I have interviewed for 10 or more head football coaching positions and got five of them. If it weren't for those recruiting allegations and the negative media behind it, I believe I would have gotten even more. I interview well because I am organized, coachable and a good communicator. Communicating is my strength. John Maxwell suggested that we master our strengths and not focus as much on our weaknesses.

One weakness of the education system is the emphasis that is put on hiring a head high school football coach and the process in which it takes place. I could give you several examples of schools that got it right, but you won't know those schools or coaches. An example to which you can relate, though, is that of Nick Saban at Alabama. He was the right fit at the right time.

When I sit down with district leaders, such as school superintendents, they communicate their concern for the lack of emphasis placed on education. When their head football coaching position is vacant the community often shows an eagerness to hire someone immediately; whereas, most are not concerned with the vacant history, English, science and social studies positions.

When I interviewed at Lawton Chiles High School, I met four other applicants. This was awkward and unprofessional, but unfortunately common. When it was my turn, the interview committee members had me sit at the end of a long table in a conference room. Around the table sat an English teacher, a guidance counselor, two parents, two players, a community leader and the athletic director. Years later I realized all committees asked similar questions in almost the same order. I will have those questions for you in a later chapter.

After the interview, I went in to see the principal's secretary before I was scheduled to speak to the principal. One of my tricks when I interview is to remember everyone's name and call them by their name at least once during the interview. I went in to talk to the principal, and he was in a full leg cast. He had broken his leg in a skiing accident. We had a great conversation. A couple days later, I was asked to come back and interview with the athletic director one-on-one.

I was super excited to get a second interview. The athletic director told me that he was concerned I had too much offense on my resume. My response was as an offensive coordinator, I study a different defense every week. I left the meeting thinking that I hoped I had made it hard for them. The next day I received a phone call from the athletic director telling me I didn't get the job, but he wanted me to come on as assistant head coach or as a coordinator. It was true ambivalence. I was disappointed and happy at the same time. However, I couldn't take the job as an assistant. I was going to take a pay cut to be their head coach as it was. It would not have been wise to leave Thomasville High School and go to Lawton Chiles High School to do the same job for less money.

A few days later I found out who they hired. This guy had won two state championships in the '80s as a head football coach. He got in some sort of trouble and wasn't allowed to coach for a while, but his punishment was over. Ironically, he had the same last name as the principal's secretary and happened to be present when the principal hurt himself on the ski trip. They were best friends.

That's how this all works sometimes. I have occupied both sides of that coin. I have interviewed for a job knowing I already had it. I have interviewed for a job and was told by the committee and the principal I had it, only to have the superintendent go in a different direction. I have also interviewed for jobs that were already decided. That's part of it.

That spring, Coach Marsh took our staff to Wofford College to their annual coaching clinic. Wofford is one of the most respected football programs in one of the most respected conferences. At the time, Coach Mike Ayers was starting his 20th season at Wofford. Several wing-t and flexbone coaches would meet up in Spartanburg, South Carolina, to learn from the master of doing more with less.

During the clinic, I ran into Welton Coffey. Coach Coffey was a great man of God who happened to be an exceptional coach. I first met him when I was thinking about coaching in Valdosta with Rick Darlington. Coach Coffey and Coach Marsh had worked on the same staff in Valdosta and were very similar in their beliefs and philosophies. Coach Coffey was with a group of coaches from Camden County, Georgia, an up-and-coming South Georgia powerhouse. Rutherford had beaten Camden so badly a few years earlier that I didn't understand what all the fuss was about.

As I did my research, though, I found out that Camden had a turf field, their weightroom was bigger than any high school gymnasium I had ever seen, they took care of their coaches in every way possible, and they had one of the top coaches in the state, Jeff Herron, as their head coach. Coach Coffey told me that they were looking for a coach. He said two of their coaches had just left and that they had filled one spot and were looking to fill the other. Stacy Stewart spoke to me about the first vacant position months earlier at a coaching clinic, but I wasn't interested; this time I was, but what do I do?

It's more money. I could coach offense or defense, and the Chiles Athletic Director said more defense on my resume would help me land a head coaching job. Tough decision. Do I move my family again - this time even further away from our families? Our two children are the only grandchildren. Our parents would not like that at all. I told them that I would pray about it and get back to them

Whenever making these decisions, I read Proverbs 16:9.

Proverbs 16:9

I was flattered, but I decided to stay in Thomasville. I enjoyed the coaching staff, the school staff, the city, our church, and I would get to call the plays during the upcoming season because the other offensive coordinator was leaving for another job. During the next few weeks, however, I realized Coach Marsh wanted our offensive line coach to call the plays instead of me. This really hurt me. I learned a lot from the situation, though. Later, when I became a head coach, I tried to make sure that all coaches' roles were clearly defined. In later chapters you will see how I did that, and how I still do it today. If I wasn't going to be able to call the plays, and I was going to continue to coach wide receivers in a run-first, run-second, run-third offense, I thought about calling the coaches at Camden County High School to see if that job was still available.

Coach Marsh knew something about me that I didn't know. He knew I was nowhere near ready to call plays. I didn't even know the difference between an even and an odd front. I didn't know our blocking schemes, and I definitely couldn't make game-time adjustments. Coach Marsh is one of my closest friends to this day, but when I left, he was not happy.

Camden County Wildcats! You talk about big time high school football. At the time, Camden was on the way to becoming what Hoover, Alabama, had become, what Lakeland, Florida, had become, what Colquitt County, Georgia, had become. In college, I went to a high school game in Texas, and it blew my mind. This was Camden every week. It was incredible.

Coach Herron asked me to bring my wife to the second interview. Before we walked in, I asked her not to act mesmerized by the weightroom and the 200-seat team meeting room. I said, "Just act like you don't see it, and don't make a big fuss." We walked in, and like flies to a light, we both had our faces pressed against the glass in awe of the facilities. This was my second interview with Coach Herron, but he had told me already that the job was mine. He was professional and treated my wife with dignity, respect and class. When the interview was over, he walked us out of his office to a realtor who was waiting to show us houses in the nearby country club.

We drove less than a mile from the school into a country club called Laurel Lakes, which houses a golf course designed by Fred Couples. The realtor informed us that seven Camden County football coaches lived in Laurel Lakes, and she would like us to join them. We had a home in Thomasville that we wanted to sell before buying another. One of the Camden coaches named Stacey Stewart bought the house for us from a coach who was leaving for another job. We rented the house from Coach Stewart. That season, we went 11-2, losing to Lowndes High School in the semifinals under the Georgia Dome. I met so many people and had so much fun, but I was bored and confused about what direction my life should take. The next season, I worked full time for Fellowship of Christian Athletes while Camden won its second state championship.

I truly enjoyed full-time sports ministry, but an encounter with Dr. Jeff Duke in Kansas City, Missouri, changed my way of thinking once again. Dr. Duke is one of the foremost experts regarding the cultural influence of the coaching profession in our society. You may know him from his facilitations on *3Dimensional Coaching*. If you haven't read his book, you should pick it up. It's incredible. He mentions one of my teams in the book and talks about the amazing job our assistants did to create a culture that changed the entire community.

Dr. Duke knew who I was because I had met one of his sons years earlier at an FCA camp where I was the speaker. Cameron Duke is one of the top young coaches in central Florida, where he is applying the same principles he learned years ago as a student assistant under Bobby Bowden. Dr. Duke pulled me to the side, and we talked about influence and culture. He asked me why I was working for FCA and not coaching. I told him that I knew God had called me to help young men better themselves in every way, not just as athletes. He said the same thing to me that Coach Herron said months later, "Why can't you do both?"

Dr. Duke told me he was on a crusade to coach the coaches. His goal was to train coaches to become much more than "X and O coaches;" he wanted to work with the whole person. He said, "Willie, you already do that. Therefore, you need to coach." He believed I would have a greater impact as a coach than I would working on staff with FCA.

Just like that, I was back on the sidelines. This time I was the athletic director and head football coach at Jefferson County High School in Monticello, Florida. Looking back on it, this was one of my favorite jobs. My wife was the guidance counselor, and I was able to hire an amazing staff. We took over a team that had won only one game the previous season and had scored only 64 points. Our defensive coordinator, Tyrone Bolware, later became an athletic director and now works as an administrator. Our offensive coordinator, Jeremy Brown, is now a successful head football coach, and ironically, I hired Dr. Duke's son, who has proven to be an amazing head coach.

We went on to have a great season, and I was named coach of the year by the Tallahassee Democrat. On the field, we were solid; off the field, things were shaky. I was the athletic director with no planning period. Our facilities were five miles from the school. I was making $30,000 less than I made at my previous two jobs. My wife was the guidance counselor of five schools, but her salary didn't reflect that. The school system was one of the worst in the country, and the things I was told in the interview never came to fruition.

This was no one's fault. When Urban Meyer called Lou Holtz complaining about the Bowling Green job, Coach Holtz told him if it was a good job, they wouldn't be interested in you.

What I have learned is your first job is probably not going to be the best job. All dogs have their share of fleas, meaning no job is perfect, but to get that great job, you may have to crawl before you walk. The best job would have these characteristics in this order of importance:

1. Athletes - You don't need five-star athletes. You need athletes that are equal to the athletes your competition has.
2. Supportive administration - Leadership that supports

you publicly and privately is vital. They leave you alone, trust you, support you and show their loyalty by giving you what you need to succeed. The relationship between a principal and a head football coach is like a marriage. Your conversations may get heated, but when you both leave the room, you're on the same page.

3. Salary - Making good money is important, but the more you make, the more you will spend. Don't let money be the reason you take a job. It should be a part of the decision-making process, but not the entire reason to take a job. When I was at Camden County we had some assistant coaches who made more than $70,000. With a salary that high, it is difficult to take a head football coaching position that pays less.

4. Adequate schedule - Perception is reality. Set your schedule up so that you can win the emotional games. Those are the games your fan base wants you to win the most. Get the most rest before those games: schedule a bye week or a weaker opponent. Manipulate your schedule to give yourself an advantage. I told a coach at Alabama State that his fans didn't know the difference between Edward Waters and Kennesaw State. At Camden County, we played eight home games a year. What an advantage. As a head coach, I often beat our rival because of the way we scheduled.

5. Adequate assistants - Every year that I won Coach of the Year I had great assistants. They were humble hard workers who cared about children.

6. Money - If you have supportive administration you can raise as much money as you need. Schedule home games you know you can win: this will create a culture of happiness which causes people to want to come to games and contribute toward your fundraising efforts.

7. Equipment - Whatever sport you are coaching, find out what other colleges are using, and use the same brand.

8. Facilities - Equipment needs to be modern and functional. You can make them pretty, but functionality is most important.

Chapter 4
The Four C's of a Conducive Culture

When hiring a new coach I use four C's to help me determine if they are the right fit. Eddie Taylor from South Georgia shared this strategy with one of my teams years ago. He stressed the importance of each principle, and I have used them ever since. I am big on professional development. If you calculate all the practice time you put in, compared to the actual assessment or game, you would realize you are big on professional development, also. I may appear more intentional, but we all benefit from professional development. The problem is, we don't realize its value, and therefore, we fail to invest in these opportunities.

The Four C's:

Character

Once we hire a coach, his or her character is attached to our program. If the coach gets arrested for driving under the influence, the headline may very well say, "High school football coach arrested for DUI." I encourage our coaches to always have extra shirts with them in their vehicles. If they want to stop by the bar on the way home, they should not be wearing our sideline polo. Perception is reality. If we lose a game and a coach decides to have two drinks at a nearby bar, it could be perceived as an attempt to drown his sorrows before driving home. Coach Jeff Herron at Camden County taught us that a bad teacher is always a bad coach. If coaches are late for work, they will be late for meetings.

31

> **Show me how you do anything, and I will show you how you do everything.**

If they lie, cheat and steal in their everyday lives, they will do the same in their coaching lives. Deion Sanders once said that whoever you are without money and influence, you will be with money and influence, just multiplied. I tell our coaches that if they show me how they do anything, I will show them how they can do everything.

> **Our true substance is revealed when we are squeezed.**

If a coach has questionable character he will not contribute to a thriving culture. Bad character rears its ugly head whenever adversity hits. When things don't go his or her way you will find out what they are truly made of. Our true substance is revealed when we are squeezed.

Chemistry

My son is a science whiz. He will tell you that there are certain elements you can use that will cause an eruption. Do you want to make a science project volcano explode? Do you want to make your project erupt, then settle down, then erupt again? Kenneth has the ability to do all of that. My son knew of Bill Nye before he knew about the Ninja Turtles, Fortnite, Lebron James or Jay Z. Kenneth understood how to make something blow up. When it comes to building a staff, I believe you need to know how to make sure things don't blow up. The wrong chemistry can cause a major explosion.

Do you have a person in your organization that no one likes? You know that person who causes everyone to tense up with anxiety because no one likes to be around them. I'm talking about the person that isn't missed when they go out of town. If a person disrupts the chemistry, you have to let them go. Their coaching talent, connections and name are not worth it in the long term if they disrupt the chemistry of your staff.

Remember just because a person is a good employee or has talent doesn't mean they are the right fit. Whenever you apply for a position, you must ask yourself, "Am I the right fit?" Do my experiences, background, personality, race, gender, beliefs and work ethic fit this organization?

Sydney Smith made popular the idiomatic expression "square peg in a round hole." Make sure you are the right fit, and make sure those who you hire are right for your organization.

Theodor Giesel started out as a novelist but was a much better fit as a children's author. We all know him as Dr. Seuss.

Oprah Winfrey started out as a news anchor and found she was a much better fit as a talk show host.

Nick Saban is a great coach, but he is not a great fit for the National Football League.

She may be a good teacher, just not for this school. He may be a good server, just not at this restaurant. He may be a good supervisor, just not for this company. He may be a good deacon, just not at this church. There are several ways to recognize a bad fit. One way is to look at the attitude.

A person who is always negative is not good for your culture. They don't have to always agree, but there has to be a positive tone when they communicate. You don't want a room full of "yes men" or robots. You want a room full of people on the same page of the same book when they leave the room.

Calling

This sounds spiritual, and it may be for some. However, it has more to do with knowing you are supposed to work in an organization. It would prove difficult to work in the medical profession if you don't like being around sick people. A person who has a dislike for children should not apply for a job as an educator or coach. If you have sticky fingers, don't work in a bank. If you have a drinking problem, don't serve as a bartender. If you don't like talking to people, sales may not be the best occupation.

Statistics on American graduates suggest that more than 70 percent of them work outside their declared field of study. Some people discover who they really are between the ages of 18 and 25. Once a person realizes what he or she is wired to do, they can find work in that field. They can find a way to make a living doing that very thing. A person who is working in their calling doesn't look at their watch to see if it is time to go home.

> **When you operate in your calling doing extra becomes normal.**

When you operate in your calling, you make "doing extra" the norm. My wife Tanika and I love to read. Therefore, our children love to read. They probably read 25 books a year. This is not extra reading; it's our normal lifestyle. When you do something you enjoy, you don't mind doing it more and more.

Competent

Someone approached me one day and asked if my staff was full. I told the individual that we had enough to get the job done but can always add someone who is the right fit. He knew I was a man of faith, and he knew faith was an integral part of my coaching. Like my race and gender, my faith is part of who I am. This gentleman went on to tell me about this "great man of God." He told me about his church attendance, how he gave money to the poor, how he volunteered at homeless shelters, how he was a deacon at his church and how he was very knowledgeable of the Bible.

When he paused to take a breath, I responded by saying, "Sounds like a great guy." He then suggested I hire him on my staff. I asked him where he currently coached, and he told me he didn't coach. I then asked where he had coached in the past. He told me he was not a coach. I went on to tell him that we already had a Chaplain, and I didn't understand why he brought this man to my attention. He said because he is a Christian, and you are a Christian.

This gentlemen didn't understand my hiring process. I often say I want to hire good men who happen to be football coaches. I offered the man in question a volunteer spot on our freshmen team, but in order to work on our varsity staff, I explained that you have to be competent. This means that you know what you are doing. You are knowledgeable in a particular area. Just because you played doesn't mean you can coach, and likewise, if you haven't played, it doesn't mean you can't coach. However, you have to be in the profession, attend clinics, sit down with coaches and prove yourself competent. Have you honed your craft? Have you improved as a coach? Have you spent time perfecting your indy period? These are things a competent coach will do.

One of the hardest functions of a leader is pruning or firing an employee. I have had to do it close to 10 times. I don't like it at all. I had to fire five coaches, including a childhood friend, at Carver. However, the four C's, my coaching packet and documentation make this difficult process go as smoothly as possible.

Chapter 5
Culture Recruits Itself

In the spring of 2012, I was hired as the next head football coach at Escambia High School in Pensacola, Florida. This is the school that produced Emmitt Smith and Trent Richardson, but they had not had much success as a football program in recent years.

Legendary Coach Dwight Thomas coached Emmitt and had success, and years later, Coach Ronnie Gilliland experienced success as well. However, the school only had three conference championships in school history and was 2-8 the season before I took over. In less than three years, we became one of the top-ranked teams in the State of Florida.

How were we able to have success so fast? We created a culture conducive to learning and growth. This change of environment impacted the entire school and community.

During the interview process, the committee emphasized the need to change the culture. Although winning football games was part of the formula, they wanted someone who would change the perception of Escambia High School. Before you take over a job in any field, it is important to learn about the history of the organization. This is easy to do with the Internet, but it is also important to talk to people in the community and those who have spent time in the organization.

The Escambia Gators used to be the Escambia Rebels and experienced violent race riots is the mid-1970s. I was the first African-American football coach in school history and only the second in the entire county.

The first African-American football coach since integration was wrongfully terminated and asked me not to take the job, but I didn't listen. When I lost my job for alleged recruiting violations and gross insubordination, I never mentioned race as a reason for my termination. I understood the ramifications of bringing up race, and as a black man I had experienced racism before. Discrimination and unfair treatment is part of the fabric that makes up our society. Not just for blacks, but for several groups in the United States. The players I allegedly recruited were all black and not allowed to play that season. Whereas the six white players, who also transferred to Escambia during the same period, were never questioned.

There was once a white quarterback in the city that played and started at four schools in four years, but never missed any games or received any punishment.

Although more than 40 local pastors, two school board members, several teachers, parents, alumni and students asked the superintendent to use progressive discipline, or transfer me to another school, he did not budge, and I lost my job. Several district employees who did much worse did not lose their jobs.

Things are harder for African-American men in almost every profession. This is not an excuse, but a reality.

Could you imagine me telling my wife that giving birth to our two children and being a woman is not so difficult? No matter how hard I try I will never know what it is like to be a woman. I could study and become the greatest gynecologist in the world, and I will never know what it is like to live as a female because I am not one.

The same is true of living as an African-American man in America. I could tell you stories about issues I know my white counterparts have never had to deal with. One night when I came out of my office, a police officer pulled a gun on me and told me there was no way I was the head football coach, and if I lied again she would have to arrest me.

Of the 129 college football head coaches at the NCAA Division I Football Bowl Subdivision level, only 13 are black

37

or African-American. I have served as the first black head football coach at three schools. I don't like talking about race, but I feel I need to in order to help you understand all the aspects and ramifications of creating a new culture. When you are successful, confident, foreign and different, people feel threatened.

In 2003, author Michael Lewis wrote a book on baseball economics titled *Moneyball*. Eight years later this book became a movie. In the movie, actor Arliss Howard plays the role of Boston Red Sox Owner John Henry. Henry had a conversation with a front office executive named Billy Beane, played by Brad Pitt. Beane was a forward thinker, ahead of his time. He used analytics to analyze players, which was a major paradigm shift. There was one scene in the movie that sums up my experience at Escambia and will help you navigate through creating a thriving culture in a lazy climate.

> **The first one through the wall gets bloody.**

These were his words:

I know you've taken it in the teeth out there, but the first guy through the wall ... it always gets bloody, always.

It's the threat of not just the way of doing business, but in their minds, it's threatening the game. But really what it's threatening is their livelihoods. It's threatening their jobs. It's threatening the way that they do things. And every time that happens, whether it's government or a way of doing business or whatever it is, the people are holding the reins, have their hands on the switch. They go crazy. I mean, anybody who's not building a team right and rebuilding it using your mode, they're dinosaurs.

That scene sums up the climate in which I found myself.

Escambia is located on the low socioeconomic west side of town and is made up of the lowest performing students in the city. According to SchoolDigger.com, the feeder middle school was ranked 884 out of 997 middle schools in the state. Most of the schools ranked below our feeder school are alternative schools or detention centers. Our job was much bigger than winning football games: we had to change the mentality of the players, students, teachers and fans. We had to change the culture and create a new one.

The coach before me, along with an assistant coach, was arrested on campus for obstruction of justice. They were accused of getting involved in a situation involving two players and the police. Three years later, one of the young men involved committed suicide. Another young man, associated with the team and known as D-Man, was murdered months before I was hired. Although this was not a norm, it gives you a sense of the culture. Out of all the high schools in the area, the perception to the public was that no student would choose to attend Escambia. The consensus was that students went to EHS because they had no other choice. Unfortunately, it seemed that teachers, stakeholders, fans and administrators had accepted, and adopted, this way of thinking. It was everywhere you looked. It was embedded in the culture. The bar was so low that I referred to our culture as a celebration of mediocrity.

The first thing I did was use the four C's to hire good coaches. I wanted a couple coaches who played at Escambia and knew what it meant to be a Gator. Coach Mike Davis was an alum who married an alum and was a member of the state championship team. He also was the head girls softball coach, and that team was by far the most successful team on campus. Davis had coached football for many years but had taken the previous season off because he did not agree with the direction of the program. Mike was a quiet guy who previously had success with the offense I brought in and exemplified the characteristics found in the four C's. On top of that, I had a feeling he would be loyal. Loyalty is the most valuable trait to a winning culture.

I was hired three days before spring break. I didn't

Loyalty is the most valuable trait to a winning culture.

39

have time to meet with the previous staff or potential coaches before the break, but I looked forward to that opportunity when we returned to school. Over the break I decided to paint the weightroom. While I washed down the walls and put blue paint tape up, I heard a knock at the door. It was Mike Davis, but not the Mike Davis I mentioned in the previous paragraph. This Mike Davis had a better tan. He was African-American, or black. He was a volunteer coach who was retired from the military. He introduced himself and asked if I could use some help. Ten minutes later, the light-skinned, or as I had him saved in my phone, "White Mike Davis" showed up. There I was with my first two coaches painting the weightroom. It was the Mike and Mike Show, featuring Willie Spears!

Their willingness to help showed me that they were the sort of men I wanted to be around. In order to change the culture around you, you have to have a staff willing to do whatever it takes to get the job done. These two gentlemen were not just good people, they were competent in different areas. I always try to hire coaches who know more than I know, who are strong in an area where I am weak - humble men who are positive, love kids and struggle with their priorities. This sounds sad, but I want coaches who consider football a calling, a passion. Someone who feels bad because they spend more time on football than on anything else.

Thomas Williams was selected as our defensive coordinator, and he would bounce things off his former high school teammate Tyrone Bolware. Thomas, or T.J., and Tyrone, or Bo, were guys from Panama City. They played at Rutherford High School a couple years ahead of me and were much better players than I was. I knew if we started the season at 0-5 that these guys would remain loyal. They were homeboys, and we had history together. Bo was my defensive coordinator at Jefferson County, where we won the conference championship and were two games away from the state championship. T.J. was my defensive coordinator at Suwannee, and we were teammates in high school and college.

The foundation of our staff was complete, but in football the most important hire is the offensive line coach. I got lucky with the next two hires, one of which was our offensive line coach Joseph Gaddy. Coach Gaddy and defensive back Coach Donte Sheppard turned out to be the catalyst to our intentional effort to change our team perception.

Coach Sheppard and Coach Gaddy are a few years younger than I am. They have insight that I don't have. They are more in tune with what our players like and what they don't like. When they suggested we use social media to promote our program, I thought it was a bad idea. The way I chose to run the program can be described as a democracy, not a dictatorship. Our coaches had the freedom to try new ideas and explore new concepts. Their suggestion to use social media changed our culture. Another thing that gave us a great advantage was professional development.

Every year I would sit down with at least 10 professional, college, high school, middle school and even youth league coaches and ask them 20 questions:

1. How do you deal with discipline?
2. How do you raise money?
3. How do you hire coaches?
4. How do you deal with parents?
5. How do you develop leaders?
6. How do you improve academics?
7. How do you handle college recruiting?
8. Describe your strength and conditioning program?
9. How would you describe your culture?
10. How long do you plan to be here?
11. Walk me through a typical game week and a typical 12-month calendar.
12. What do you do if a player misses practice?
13. How is your relationship with your athletic director?
14. Tell me about your booster club.
15. Where does this job rank of all the places you've been and why?
16. What do you run on offense and why?

17. What do you run on defense and why?
18. How much time do you spend on special teams?
19. Do your players play both ways?
20. How important is winning to you?

During my second year at Escambia I was scheduled to speak to all the eighth-graders in Montgomery, Alabama. I had no idea that five years later I would be the head football coach in that same city. While in town for a week of speaking events, I visited Huntingdon College, Alabama State University, Faulkner University and Prattville High School. I sat down with a coach from each of these schools and asked those 20 questions.

Coach Turk at Huntingdon gave me the simplest advice when I asked him how they led the country in offense the previous season. He said coach, if there are seven in the box, we run it; if there are eight, we pass it. This was something I already knew but had never considered in that way. We used that the following year at Escambia and led the nation in rushing offense.

An assistant coach at Prattville High School taught me how to get a discount on pallets of Whey Protein and told me about their gridiron girls. Those two concepts changed our program at Escambia. This enabled us to give our players a scoop of protein after every workout. Our team was mostly made up of students who received free and reduced-price lunches. Most of their parents could not afford to provide proper nutrition. Therefore, we needed to give them at least eight ounces of protein each day on top of what they normally consumed. High school athletes burn calories and need to build muscle. No matter how effective you think your workouts should be, if an athlete is not receiving proper nutrition, you are working against yourself. Fast food, potato chips, fruit drinks and other sweets do not build muscle. They actually work against what we are trying to do. The days of giving athletes a Snickers bar and a Coke are over.

When the Prattville coach told me about their gridiron girls, it gave me an idea. I had several teachers tell me that they saw a change in several of our football players and that they wished there was a way to see the same change in some of our girls. So we came up with the Gator Girls and the Gatorettes. These groups would have to abide by the same rules as the boys, as far as discipline, academic excellence and hard work. The Gatorettes was a dance group of which I was in charge. If the girls misbehaved we didn't allow them to dance. The Gator Girls were ambassadors of our program and promoted the high school by doing several things including giving visitors campus tours, organizing functions, promoting football and preparing packages.

We gave members of each group the gear they needed, as well as access and prestige. What they did for us was unprecedented. We were the first team in the panhandle to have a Twitter and Snapchat account. These 25 girls posted pictures on several social media outlets. One of the members ran the Snapchat page. Coach Sheppard ran the Facebook page, and Coach Gaddy ran the Twitter page. We figured out early on that players like to see pictures of themselves. We had five to 10 girls taking photos each day at practice. These pictures, as well as graphics and posters made by different friends of the program, were used on all the social media outlets. My college friend Erin took our program to another level with her computer graphics talent.

The key was creating a buzz. This buzz caused us to triple our fundraising budget. When people are excited about your product, you can sell more merchandise, charge for parking and even charge companies to say their names over the public address system. Imagine 25 girls posting three football pictures a day, along with quotes, schedules and words about the program. No one knew that they were Gator Girls or Gatorettes. By doing this, we got information out to more than 500,000 people a day because of the rule of 72. This is a finance principle that works with social media.

We had 165 football players and 50 girls. That's more than 200 people posting three pictures a day for their followers to view. We started selling advertising packages to businesses because we could prove that our social media pages received more traffic than radio or television stations in our local area. The analytics were off the charts. If each student has 2,500 unique followers, you can reach 500,000 people per day. Officials from Florida Atlantic University called and asked us to teach them how to get the most out of their social media presence.

During our time at Escambia High School, we also made significant improvements to the fieldhouse facilities. When I was hired, the Escambia football weightroom facility had outdated equipment and no school funding to make improvements. We led an overhauled Football Booster Organization to raise $35,000 to remodel the facility. We also were instrumental in working with the Escambia County School District in the remodeling and designing of the football facility lobby, head coach's office, assistant coaches' office, equipment room and locker room.

We placed significant emphasis on academics. When we arrived in March 2012, we released 40 players for behavior violations and low grade point averages. Eight of these players were varsity starters, and one of them had a Division I Football Championship Subdivision offer.

To ensure players remained eligible, we instituted an after-school program, requiring students who earned below a 2.5 grade point average to attend tutoring sessions. We enlisted volunteers from the community and faculty to tutor our athletes. We also read to the students regularly and required daily independent reading of each student. We modeled literacy strategies and emphasized academics in our parent and booster meetings. We often invited administrators to present academic information to parents at these events. Our players were instrumental in participating in elementary school literacy programs. These academic efforts resulted in a 50 percent increase in reading learning gains among our football players

Only seven players were ineligible in the spring of 2014. Three of our players were inducted into the EHS Hall of Fame, an accomplishment that had not occurred since 2009. By spring 2014, a two-year total of 26 players, the most in Escambia High School history, had signed letters of intent to play college football. We accomplished this by communicating with 100 colleges per player, according to each of their abilities. Although all players did not receive full scholarships, each player received an opportunity to continue their education and playing career.

We revitalized excitement and school spirit at EHS. We literally went door to-door and asked people to come to our games. Before we arrived, the team averaged $2,500 at the gate for each game. When we left, they averaged $6,500 per gate per game. We created a social media identity, which was nonexistent before our arrival, for the program.

The staff we hired at EHS exhibited leadership not only in football but also in our school's professional learning communities, behavior intervention programs, and exceptional student education programs. One administrator said that the influence we had on the entire student body outreached the influence that football alone had on the student body. Many students have acknowledged spiritual changes through the Fellowship of Christian Athletes.

The most significant accomplishments that we made were not on the gridiron. When I was hired in March 2012, according to Maxpreps, the Gators were ranked 317 in Florida. At the time of my wrongful termination on September 17, 2014, the Gators were ranked 17th in the state. We made great gains during the 2013 football season. Five players made the all-state team in 2013. This was only the second time this honor occurred in EHS history; EHS defeated rival schools in the same regular season for the first time in more than 30 years. Maxpreps reported that in 2013, the Gators had the No. 1 rushing offense in the country and the No. 1 running back, Danikeei Hollowell, who never played a whole game, in the state. When we were hired, the Gators were ranked last in district 1-6A. When we left, we were No. 1 in almost every category.

We completely created a new culture. Our outside-the-box methods took us to another level, but also caused our opponents to work harder at tearing our program down, instead of actually working harder on building their programs up.

We were the first team in the Panhandle to have a Twitter page. We were doing satellite camps three years before Jim Harbaugh. We had barbers come to our school and cut our players' hair before Oregon, Alabama or any other college had barbershops on campus. We filmed a show in a barbershop before Lebron James and Nick Saban. We had two videos go viral on footballscoop.com. We were several years too early, maybe, but since our departure, several school, district and state regulations have been changed to catch up to our innovative approach to culture. The way we got players to buy in to the program also was innovative. We tapped into their need for entitlement and recognition.

We told the players if they made every workout in the summer, we would put their names on the backs of their jerseys. We put 15 players' photos on billboards across the city. We had a social media-based sports show, a radio show and a weekly newsletter. We had music at our practices and games. We had a day, similar to Alabama's program, for eighth-graders who were already registered to go to our school. We patterned our program after colleges.

In three years, we had more than 25 players transfer to our school to play football. Like most cities, players move around and transfer often for a number of reasons. The local coaches got together and said I was recruiting players. I ultimately lost my job, and I still have not recovered. However, when I say culture recruits itself I am not only talking about players, I'm talking about stakeholders, boosters, fundraisers, parents, fans, teachers and religious leaders.

When I lost my job, more than 700 people came to the school board meeting - evidence of the culture we had created. When I visited Pensacola years later, the people were still talking about the impact we made - evidence of the culture we created. We had players who were scheduled to receive a special diploma because of their lack of attendance but ended up with a standard diploma - evidence of the culture we created.

We did not give our players locks to lock up their

personal items. We told them that we would not have success if we could not trust one another. Believe it or not, items did not go missing in our locker room - evidence of the culture we created. Our freshmen team went from no wins in two seasons to 23 wins in three seasons - evidence of the culture we created. Our varsity team had six players on the all-state team - evidence of the culture we created. I was named coach of the year - evidence of the culture we created. I was nominated teacher of the year, even though I didn't technically teach a class - evidence of the culture we created.

Our players had no problem coming in three times a day, once before school for 90 minutes, during class for 90 minutes and after school for two hours. I learned this from a visit I had with Coach Bill Clark. I realized we had a team made up of level-one players, or players who had some sort of learning disability or streak of laziness. We figured if we did more teaching and less screaming we could play faster with more confidence. This worked as we simplified our playbook, put our best players on defense and put starters on special teams. The culture we created allowed us to have success.

When I provide professional development to churches, I use statistics provided by the Barna Group to emphasize the average age of most church congregations. This leads us into the importance of training young people to replace the older people. It's actually that simple. In sports, we have the same issue. The sooner you can teach them your culture the better. At Escambia, we did this during the summer. In the summer, I asked all players to bring their little brothers, cousins, friends and neighbors. I didn't care if they were football players or not. I knew that having them participate in our summer program had the potential to change their lives. We used this time to teach them our culture.

They learned that we don't lean over during conditioning, doesn't matter if you are 7 years old or a three-year starter. They learned that we don't use profanity. They learned that we hold each other accountable. They learned that we have fun: every Thursday we played some sort of fun competitive game, such as dodgeball. They learned that part

47

of our culture was to get them ready for life after football. They learned how to change a tire and tie a tie. Many of them came from fatherless homes. Therefore, we felt the need to teach them skills that a man would teach, if he were present. We taught them how to order a steak and how to properly shake someone's hand. We taught them how to write a check, write a resume and do an interview. We also tried to teach them that their faith and their family should come before their sport. We did this by starting each day off with a devotion from our Chaplain.

I believe hiring Glenn Bousquet and Bob Govoni was the smartest thing I ever did. The lighter Mike Davis suggested I hire Coach Bousquet. He became my ace. He and Bob Govoni, who we called Preach, both graduated from Escambia. Preach was our Chaplain. It was his job to make sure the coaches and players had someone to talk to when they experienced tragedy. His job description was to make sure I grew spiritually because I was the head coach. That position gave me the most influence and responsibility. With that came great expectations. Coach Thomas was our defensive coordinator, and Preach was our spiritual coordinator. Glenn Bousquet was our unofficial program coordinator.

His wisdom was exactly what I needed. However, I didn't know it at first. The first thing that stood out to me was his passion for his alma mater and his unique ability to relate to our freshmen players. Growing up on the west side of Pensacola, attending Escambia and spending more than 20 years in the military, ultimately retiring as a major in the United States Marine Corps Field Artillery, prepared him to handle 65 ninth graders from the worse feeder school in the city. Coach suggested that we stop teaching them how to lift weights and start teaching them organization skills, study habits and life management skills. I told him that we could not take off a whole semester from lifting. Then he asked me how many freshmen were ineligible after our first year. I said close to 40. He said, "I bet they were strong, though."

His point was that we had to change the culture

academically when it came to our approach with our freshmen. I listened to him, and the following year we had less than 10 players ineligible.

Coach Bousquet worked at our feeder middle school. Those students could go to our school or our rival's school. He did such a great job of building relationships with those students that our rival school canceled their freshman season.

I have received four genuine jaw-dropping compliments in my life. One of them came from Coach Bousquet. He told me that he had served our country in the military for several years, and he had been a part of sports teams longer than I had lived. He went on to say that he had never met a leader as organized and equipped to lead as I was. He is not a man to throw out compliments. He actually thought they made a mistake hiring me before he met me. So for him to say that blew my mind and humbled me.

I joined an on-campus teachers' book club, attended band and choir performances, had our players read to elementary students, volunteered to teach classes on every hallway and made sure I was at every faculty meeting. I also encouraged teachers

In order to change a culture you have to change, compromise and care.

to treat football players the same way they treated other students by not showing any preferential treatment. This behavior was unusual for a football coach, but not for me. In order to change a culture, you have to change, compromise and care.

Chapter 6
What Teachers Can Learn from Coaches

Essential Strategies

What students want:
1. Recognition
2. Working systems and tools
3. A teacher who cares about them as a person, not a student

How to deal with low achievers:
1. Provide scheduled evaluations.
2. Don't allow them to negatively affect high performers.
3. Realize if they fail, you fail. You're in this together.

Satisfied students contribute to a healthy culture:
1. Clearly define expectations.
2. Set realistic individual and classroom goals.
3. Catch them doing good, and reward them for it.

Acknowledge and award success:
1. Create a system of gratitude.
2. Reward good behavior, and celebrate when goals are achieved.
3. Recognize good behavior when it gets repeated.

Make doing extra the normal thing to do:
1. Use quantitative and qualitative measurements acquired through class surveys.

2. Seek and acknowledge difference-makers.

3. Lead by example.

I have included acronyms that may help you create a classroom culture that produces intentional learners and not robots who study just to do well on the test. Most students could not care less about the materials: they are buying into you, not the product. The same is true if you are in the sales industry.

> **Significant learning does not take place without a significant relationship**

I speak to members of corporate America often, and they understand this principle. Therefore, the teacher must constantly grow and improve in his personal life and in his professional life. In the margin of this book, in your phone or on a sheet of paper, write down three personal and three professional goals.

In today's society, intellect is overrated and outdated. Instead of knowing the information, you just need to know where to find it. This causes a problem in the classroom. However, if the classroom is a harmonious gathering of people on the same team, learning can take place.

S.O.F.T.E.N.

- **S**mile
- **O**pen posture
- **F**orward lean
- **T**ouch
- **E**ye contact
- **N**od

There is a fifth-grade teacher named Barry White Jr. in Charlotte, North Carolina, who understands this principle. He starts each day greeting his students with a unique hand shake. This intentional gesture creates a culture of togetherness. Who would want to disappoint a teacher like Mr. White? The S.O.F.T.E.N. technique works and is vital in creating a thriving culture.

Smile and look each student in the eye every day. Keep an open posture. Lean forward, letting each student know that we are all in this together. Students need to know that the teacher is not a supervisor in an Armani suit, but rather, the teacher is a leader with boots, coveralls and greasy hands. It is important to make positive contact with students every day. A high-five, a hand shake, an encouraging pat on the shoulder and even a hug, when appropriate, are nonverbal forms of communication that are proven to speak loudly - without saying a word. In fact, not talking is sometimes the best form of communication. Instead, try listening to students. Students want to know that what they have to say is important. Nodding is a form of active listening.

T.E.A.M.

- **T**ogether
- **E**veryone
- **A**chieves
- **M**ore

At the end of a football game, the entire stadium can see the results of the coach's evaluation. *We* win, or *we* lose. It is never *they* lose, or *they* won. A wise coach once told me that if a team wins, all the credit should go to the players and to the assistant coaches, but if a team loses, the head coach should take the blame. This principle has worked well for me. The team approach is key when it comes to changing a culture.

Jeremy Brown, who coached with me in Jefferson County, was recognized as one of the top teachers in the state for his classroom gains in his Exceptional Student Education class, which focuses on education for students diagnosed with learning disabilities.

For the first time in history, the state decided to count

52

the students' test scores with mainstream averages. Coach Brown knew some teachers were offering pizza to students if they did their best. Others talked about having a free day in class with video games and movies. Coach Brown told his students that he needed them to do their best. They responded by saying that no one thought they were smart, so it didn't matter anyway. He told them a little fib. He said if they failed the test he would lose his job. He proceeded with this Jedi mind trick by saying they probably couldn't do it, so he should say goodbye. Not only did they do better than expected, but they were top performers in the state! Their performance was based on the TEAM culture Coach Brown had set. They did not want to let Coach Brown down. He was more than a teacher to them. He was family.

F.A.M.I.L.Y.

- **F**orget
- **A**bout
- **M**e
- **I**
- **L**ove
- **Y**ou

Nothing matters more than service. The way students get treated will make or break your classroom. When a student knows you have sacrificed your time, money and comfort for them, they will go the extra mile for you.

Do you enjoy the culture of Chick-fil-A? Many people do. I believe the reason for this is that the company is intentional about service. When I hear customer service employees say "my pleasure" as they are serving me, it makes me want to come back again and again.

Teaching is the greatest profession because teachers teach all professions. Often, however, physical education teachers don't get the same respect as classroom teachers. I have worked in more than 10 high schools, and in all but one of them, teachers would send students down to the gym every once in the awhile. A few times I was working in the gym and witnessed this happening, so I would find different students and recommend them for that particular teacher's class - sort of like returning the favor. If teachers learn to respect one another's space and positions, students win.

Teaching is the greatest profession because teachers teach all professions

When I first started speaking to educators, there was no Siri or Google, and we didn't go to the Internet to find information about everything. So, when speaking to educators, they accepted me as their equal, not just as a coach. They could read my bio, which stated I was an educator, published author and had been named teacher of the year. They also could see that I earned a postgraduate degree in education. That's all they needed to know. Years later, when the Internet gained popularity, and I had served as a head coach, people would Google me before a presentation and ask their principals why they invited a football coach to speak. The stigma of working as a coach had a negative connotation attached to it.

If you truly want to change the culture of your company or school, sit down with the custodian, secretary, coaches, teachers, cafeteria staff and maintenance workers. You can learn a lot from everyone, including the IT manager and the resident mechanic. In every school, the custodian is going to know more about student behavior than teachers. The custodian often navigates without detection. This gives them a great advantage in recognizing people's true identities.

When speaking with teachers, I use several techniques I learned as a coach. My true identity is that of an educator, which coaching falls under. Somewhere in society, though, we started associating athletics with ignorance. This is unfair and unfortunate.

Coach is a Hungarian word that comes from a mode of transportation known as horse-drawn carriage. College students in the early 19th century used the slang word to refer to a private tutor who would "drive" a student through exams, like a horse driving a passenger. The practical application of the word we use today literally means to take an individual to a place that they could not have gotten to had the two not met.

Although the words teacher and coach are synonymous, for the purpose of this chapter, when we refer to teachers, we are describing educators who work a traditional school day. When we talk about coaches, we are referring to individuals who coach student-athletes before or after a traditional school day. If you are not a teacher or coach you can still learn from the principles in this chapter and apply them to your church, civic organization, business or company.

What gets measured gets done. Effective weight loss does not happen if an individual doesn't weigh himself. Quantitative data is effective, not sufficient, but effective. While playing sports, we received instant data during

What gets measured gets done

and after our assessments. Coaches don't have the luxury of blaming parents, tests or students. If a coach loses a contest, he cannot say it was not his fault.

Comedian John Crist posted a fictitious video portraying a coach who says, "I don't know what you want me to do. Everyone says football is a team game. It's not a team game. I did my part. I put in a great game plan. These players are horrible. My players are no good."

The video is funny because no coach would say those things. However, I have heard teachers use words similar to John's in the video. In sports, the coach knows if he or she failed by looking at the score when the game is over. In the classroom, weekly assessments, end-of-course exams and grades accomplish the same thing.

Most teachers want a student like my wife. She was selected to join the first ever International Baccalaureate program in Bay County Florida. She always has excelled academically. She was the student who sat in the front row with her glasses on, pencils sharpened, book opened, ready to learn. She read the assigned chapter the night before and was eager to discuss in class what she had learned. Conversely, I was the student who did not take my books home. We were not in the same classes because she took all honors courses, and I took basic classes. We did not have any of the same teachers. I showed up late. She was on time. She sat in the front, and I sat in the back. I did enough to get by, and she did more than she was required to do. I received 53 discipline referrals in middle school. She never received a discipline referral, ever. In high school I spent many days sitting with Mrs. Hartzog during in-school suspension. My wife didn't even know where the ISS class was located.

Most teachers want to teach students like my wife because it's easier. In sports, that would be equivalent to coaching Lebron James, Tom Brady or Aaron Judge in high school, and most coaches don't have the luxury of getting a team full of top athletes. Coaches have to coach whoever shows up. The same is true for most educators.

When I left Carver High School, we had a four-star linebacker and five other players with Division I FBS offers. Montgomery, Alabama, produces amazing athletes. At Carver, we had several Division I basketball and football players. When I coached at Jefferson County, we had eight Division I athletes on a 1A team with only 250 students in the high school. But I want to use my time at Escambia High to help us understand the importance of ownership, evaluation and measurement.

At the end of every calendar quarter we would sit down as a staff and do a self-evaluation. This usually consisted of me getting on to the coaches about their slacking off during offseason. We had measurements in place to recruit students on our campus, upgrade the facility, meet with our position groups weekly and monitor players' grades. When it came to the strength and condition portion of our meeting, TJ

Williams pointed out that according to the data, we were in shape, faster and quicker, but we were not stronger.

Although we all had weightroom duty, as the head coach, I ran the weightroom during the school day, and we had not experienced gains in our core lifts of bench press, power clean and parallel back squat. I could not argue with the data. I couldn't blame the parents for not teaching their children proper lifting techniques. I couldn't blame the middle school for not having a weighlifting program. I couldn't blame cell phones, social media or entertainment. I had to look in the mirror and blame myself. I was in charge of the weightroom, and the players weren't getting stronger, point blank.

We used a system I adopted from my days at Camden County and adapted it to fit Escambia. It was called the Super Gator Test. It measured the student-athletes in 10 categories:

1. Height
2. Weight
3. Bench press
4. Power clean
5. Parallel squat
6. 40-yard dash
7. 10-yard dash
8. Bench jumps
9. Pro shuttle
10. Mile run

Each student-athlete is tested four times a year. We tell students that if they show up and try, they will see results. While serving on a Professional Learning Community committee, we analyzed data of teachers with failure rates of 80 percent or greater. In sports, coaches don't have the luxury of keeping their jobs with a failure rate that high. Coach TJ Williams pointed out that one of our lower-achieving athletes, Kory Free, scored a 0 on his bench jump test. Zero. Meaning that in 60 seconds he did not have one successful bench jump. Patrick McCovick jumped over the bench 45 times. How come we're not talking about him? The reason is because progress, learning and execution is measured in gains. That is why there is a pretest and a post test.

Two years later, Kory completed 25 jumps, and each time we tested him he improved. If he showed up every day and put in the effort but saw no improvement, that's my fault. Leadership is ownership.

Leadership is Ownership

Some of your students don't need extra help, but most do. We went from being ranked 317th to 17th because we made doing extra our normal. Our defensive staff started making the defense come in an hour before school to lift weights. We implemented that commitment for the whole team. Within six months, it became our new norm. We took over a team that had never experienced winning and changed their mindset.

We decided to put the entire football team on the weighlifting team, and although it was uncommon, we approached the weighlifting season the same as the football season. We typed the schedule up the same way and began the season with the same emphasis. We ended up going 6-1 in the weighlifting season. This paradigm shift convinced our student-athletes they were winners, and they started winning.

That fall we played against Pace High School. Their coach was Mickey Lindsey, who was Emmitt Smith's position coach when Emmitt played running back at Escambia High School. Pace was ranked 10th in the state. We were not ranked in the top 100. He is a much better coach than I am and had a more experienced

The uncommon approach is only uncommon to "un-motivate" underachievers.

staff. At half time, I had a "David and Goliath" video set up, and I told our team that Pace had more cheerleaders than we had football players. This was our first year at Escambia, and I had cut 40 players from the team, which left us with 23 varsity players at a 6A school. Coach TJ Williams told the team that we had already beat Pace in weighlifting, and those were the same players playing football.

The truth is we did not beat Pace in weighlifting. That was the one match we lost, but we counted it as a win because they won the 110-pound and the 119-pound weight class and beat us by only one point. We told our players that those weight classes were too small to count as football players, so therefore, we had won. Now, I tell you this because creative motivation is a key component to creating culture. Just like you tell your children: Santa Claus, the Tooth Fairy and the Easter Bunny are real. It is not true, but it protects their innocence for a little while and creates a safe culture of happiness while they're young.

We went on to win a game that we should have lost on the last play of the game because we had created a culture conducive to achieving the impossible. The same can happen in the classroom. Why not create an environment

> **Creative motivation is a key component to creating culture**

where all students are high achievers? All you have to do is make a test for each student that you know they will pass. This will change their perception of themselves. Set up an opportunity for them to compete with one another or against another class. If the end goal is for students to learn the materials, then there should not be any hesitation on getting out of our comfort zones in an effort to create a culture where we all succeed.

I know what you are probably thinking: of course we got the right mix of players because we were able to cut so many off the team. Remember what I said earlier, though. If a student shows up and tries, we can help them improve. If a student does not show up, or if a student does not show effort, we have to find a way to remove him from the learning environment because he could potentially become cancerous. Once a cancer spreads, it is harder to treat successfully.

Chapter 7
Head Coaches

Coaching legend Bud Wilkinson said the best coach is an organized teacher. I have learned something valuable like that from every leader who I have worked under. That goes for every pastor, every principal, every head coach and every supervisor. In some situations, I learned what not to do. While in other situations, I learned what to do if I were ever to be in that role.

Jeff Herron taught me the importance of organization. In 2007, he was the head football coach at Camden County High School In Kingsland, Georgia, and I was one of his many assistants. He hired me to coach defensive backs. The weekend before we started fall camp, he took us assistants to Tennessee for three days to talk about each phase of the football program. He issued us a 100-page binder that detailed our responsibilities and his expectations.

In this chapter, I will give you several resources that helped me organize the teams I managed. Although these materials are specifically geared for coaches, they can be formatted to fit any organization.

Each leader has to cast his vision and make it stick. The way I do this is by sharing our mission statement and philosophy. I ask the group to break both vision statements down into three words or less. This becomes our hashtag for the year. We post the mission statement, organizational philosophy and the hashtag everywhere.

MISSION STATEMENT

Our mission is to use the game of football to teach young men to be successful at home, in the classroom, in the community and in life after football, and for our program to set the bar high and be recognized as the standard of excellence in high school football throughout the state and in the country.

After reading our mission statement, Emmitt Smith shared it with NFL Films and said, "This is what it's all about."

COACHING PHILOSOPHY

Billy Graham said, "A coach will impact more people in one year than the average person will in an entire lifetime." That quote is the thesis of my coaching philosophy. I want to use that influence to build men in a world in desperate need of men. I am a head football coach because I believe it is the best way to mold future husbands, leaders, good citizens and fathers. If men would step up and be men our world would be a better place.

Several over-aged boys who call themselves men lack skill, ambition, education and substance. Two of the most powerful words ever spoken are, "Coach said."

President Kennedy quoted the Bible in one of his speeches and said, "To whom much is given, much is also required or expected." Being a head football coach is a great responsibility. It comes with immeasurable influence. We will know if we did a good job or not by the humans we run into at their 20-year reunion.

> **Bad leaders don't plan to fail, they fail to plan.**

I believe we should start with the end in mind. It should be all's well that begins well, not all's well that ends well. The first 15 days are very crucial. Use this time wisely with an initial plan. Remember, bad leaders don't plan to fail, they fail to plan.

THE FIRST 15 DAYS OF MANAGING A NEW PROGRAM

- Aggressively
- Chasing
- Excellence

ACE

Each season we will have a different theme. Themes that I have used in the past include ALL IN, Carpe Diem, Get Better, New Era, FINISH, F.A.M.I.L.Y. and Count on me.

This season, each player will strive to be the ACE, or No. 1 guy, in his position coach's eyes. Each coach will strive to be the most loyal and dependable - the head coach's ACE. The head coach will strive to be the one the principal, staff, community and players can count on - the ACE. The team will Aggressively Chase Excellence, seeking to become one of the many ACEs in the high school.

Day One   Wednesday, February 21

- Meet with principal one-on-one
- Meet with assistant principal one-on-one
- Meet with athletic director
- Greet teachers before and after school in the library (donuts & juice)
- Meet on-campus stakeholders
- Meet the team. Give them calendar for next 10 months
- Meet the staff. Give them calendar for next 10 months
- Survey all stakeholders using Google Survey
- Meet with Guidance Counselor one-on-one
- Meet with other administrators one-on-one
- Launch/relaunch social media campaign

Day Two   Thursday, February 22

- Help previous class find a college
- Meet with bookkeeper
- Meet with two assistant coaches, one-on-one
- Tour and evaluate facilities; address risk management issues
- Evaluate and make changes to website
- Evaluate inventory, make needs assessment (including equipment)
- Meet with two senior players, one-on-one
- Attend school event

Day Three   Friday, February 23

- Schedule Fellowship of Christian Athletes meeting in auditorium
- Meet with two senior football players, one-on-one
- Meet with two assistant coaches
- Send out notice for parent/booster meeting on Monday evening
- Meet with strength coach
- Meet with band director
- Fundraising meeting

Day Four   Saturday, February 24

- Meet with community leaders and potential sponsors
- Meet with local church leaders
- Meet with local business owners
- Drive around and learn the city and the neighborhoods the players come from

Day Five   Sunday, February 25

- Visit local church with family
- Eat at mom-and-pop restaurant with family
- Prepare for parent/booster meeting

- Schedule home visits

Day Six   Monday, February 26

- Super Mascot Test before school and during class
- Super Mascot Test after school for new players and those not in class
- Parent/Booster meeting at 6 p.m. in auditorium
- Monitor halls
- Chat with teachers between classes and on their planning periods
- Meet with two seniors, one-on-one
- Meet with two assistant coaches
- Attend school event

Day Seven   Tuesday, February 27

- Super Mascot Test before school and during class
- Super Mascot Test after school for new players & those not in class
- Incorporate signage throughout the facility
- Monitor halls
- Chat with teachers in-between classes and on their planning period
- Meet with two seniors
- Meet with two assistant coaches
- Attend school event
- Evaluate roster

Day Eight   Wednesday, February 28

- Super Mascot Test before school and during class
- Super Mascot Test after school for new players and those not in class
- Incorporate signage throughout the facility
- Develop spring/summer calendar
- Review helmet reconditioning situation
- Monitor halls

- Chat with teachers between classes and on their planning periods
- Meet with two seniors, one-on-one
- Meet with two assistant coaches
- Attend school event

Day Nine   Thursday, March 1

- Super Mascot Test before school and during class
- Super Mascot Test after school for new players and those not in class
- Incorporate signage throughout the facility
- Monitor halls
- Chat with teachers between classes and on their planning periods
- Meet with two seniors, one-on-one
- Meet with two assistant coaches
- Attend school event

Day 10   Friday, March 2

- Fellowship of Christian Athletes meeting in auditorium
- Meet with cheer coach
- Meet with middle school football coaching staff
- Study hall during class for players
- Search for academic coach
- Meet with guidance counselors
- Attend school event

Day 11   Saturday, March 3

- Meet with entire coaching staff, 10 a.m. to 5 p.m.

Day 12   Sunday, March 4

- May visit local church with family
- Eat at mom-and-pop restaurant with family
- Spend time in office organizing and setting up

Day 13   Monday, March 5

- Players will lift before school and during class
- There will also be a lifting group after school
- Meet with cafeteria staff
- Meet with custodians
- Coaches start meeting next week at 6 a.m. on Tuesdays and Thursdays
- Attend school event

Day 14   Tuesday, March 6

- Players will not lift before school - mid-term exams
- Players will lift during school
- There will be a lifting group after school
- Reorganize coaches' offices
- Meet with head coaches of other sports
- Attend school event

Day 15   Wednesday, March 7

- Starting 6 a.m. next Wednesday, mat drills
- Players will not lift before school - mid-term exams
- Players will lift during school
- There will be a lifting group after school
- Meet with head coaches of other sports
- Attend school event

     I give all of our coaches a binder each year, even if they were with me the previous three seasons. Everyone gets a binder.
     The following includes information inside the binder:

PROGRAM ORGANIZATION

1. Academics
2. Mentor Program
3. Liaison Team

4. Parents
5. Booster Club
6. Fundraising
7. Coaching Staff
8. Administration
9. Faculty
10. Get students into college
11. Strength and Conditioning
12. JV/Freshmen & Youth Teams
13. Equipment
14. Field Maintenance
15. Practice
16. Summer Camps
17. Game Planning
18. Game Day Organization
19. Home Games
20. Away Games
21. Media
22. Physicals
23. Forever Learning
24. Offense, Defense, Special Teams

1. Academics

The best coach is the organized teacher

We will have an academic coach who will oversee our academic program and make sure every player qualifies for college. All students with failing grades will go to mandatory study hall the entire school year. We will make sure student athletes take correct courses from the correct teachers. Different students get along with and perform better for certain teachers.

2. Mentoring Program

The mentoring program is where our student athletes

will mentor elementary school students. I have implemented this program at every school for which I was head coach. Whenever we have home games, we read to the elementary school students in an effort to invite them to the game and show them the importance of reading. The school also will benefit from genuine, positive press on social media as we give back to the community. The purpose is to develop character in young people and magnify the importance of education. The mentoring program also will teach our players a lot about the influence they have on young people and the responsibilities that comes with that.

3. Liaison Team

This is sort of a unity council. Former Congressman and former Nebraska Head Football Coach Tom Osborne was one of many coaches to use a unity council. Nebraska won seven conference championships and three national championships after implementing the program. The idea is to create a team that is greater than the sum of its individual parts or talents. The liaison team acts as a communications tool for the players and the coaching staff. The coaching staff will select members of the team, which usually consists of three seniors, two juniors, a sophomore and a freshman, if there is one on the varsity squad, but no matter what, the team needs to consist of an odd number. I will meet with them every week for a few minutes to address disciplinary issues and issues that contribute to a lack of morale and team unity.

Benefits of liaison team

- Eliminates perception of unequal treatment among players
- Players are accountable to each other for their actions, leading to positive peer pressure.
- Players take more ownership in the team and will police themselves

- Players develop a better understanding of what is acceptable and unacceptable behavior
- Morale is improved because players feel their concerns are heard
- Team unity is improved with everyone committed to a common mission

4. Parents

I have come to believe parents can be the best part - and the worst part - of your program. The relationship between a coach and parents must be that of a partnership. When it comes to their son, whether it be helping to get him into college or seeing after his health and behavior, I always will be available. When it comes to communication about playing times, we will have to find a good time for both of us. I usually don't talk to parents about playing time. I will meet with parents early to introduce myself and to let them know the direction the program is headed. I will explain the importance of appropriate communication. I will talk to them about NCAA requirements, including SAT and ACT testing. I also will share my emotional bank account discipline paradigm. I will give them my phone number, and they will know that I will treat their son as if he is my very own son. During the season I will request they talk to me on Tuesdays after practice, if they have any issues. However, I am always available for emergencies. I will remind them that they have a picture of one player on their refrigerator, and I have a picture of the entire team. Our motives are different, but that doesn't mean we can't work together.

5. Booster Club

The booster club must be aware of the goals of the football program. Members of the booster or quarterback club must know how important they are to the success of the program. If we are going to take the program into the 21st century, the booster club is going to play a major role in that renovation. It is important to follow-up parent meetings with encouragement of parents to participate in the booster club. Fundraisers must be scheduled to ensure consistent cash flow for year-round needs. The needs of the football program include, but are not limited to, things like quality video of practice and games, team media guides or programs, team shirts and shorts for players, pre-game meals, football camps, sending coaches to coaching clinics and on college visits and an awards banquet at the end of the season. I attend all booster meetings to show my support and gratitude.

6. Fundraising

Working at different schools has taught me that different fundraisers work in different places. Here are a few that have worked in the past: Discount Gold Cards, golf tournament, mini-golf tournament, bowling tournament, dodge ball tournament, corn hole tournament, bingo night fundraiser, Women's Football 101 Clinic, pancake breakfast, spaghetti dinner, cake auction, Lift-A-Thon, selling advertisements in the game programs, selling sponsorship banners that were placed around the stadium, selling a sponsorship to paint the logo on the field, car wash, Youth Camp and Combine.

7. Coaching Staff

The number one quality in a coach is not his football knowledge, not his playing experience, not his ability to teach the game, not even his resume or credentials. The

Where there is more than one vision, that's division

number one thing that I look for in a coach is his love for young men. I mean an ability to really love them. Does he drive by them in his pickup truck as they're walking home, or does he see to it that they have a ride if they need one? Does he invite them over to his house for a cookout every once in a while? Is it just a job, or does he love being a coach?

Now, those other qualities I named also are important. We use four Cs in hiring our staff: Character, Competence, Chemistry and Calling. I know what a good staff looks like, and I know what an average staff looks like. We can't have coaches who look at their watches constantly. No clock-punchers. The staff has to be loyal to the head coach. We can disagree behind closed doors, but when we walk out, we are all on the same page. Loyalty is key.

We have a coach's retreat every year. I go over my expectations for the staff, and I ask them what they expect from me. However, there is only one vision for our program. Where there is more than one vision, that's division. Our goal is not to just win football games but to help mold young men. Twenty years from now, we will know if we did a good job with the lives we were given to shape.

> **If I see rat droppings in the gym, I don't need to see the rat. The droppings are evidence the rat is there.**

8. <u>Administration</u>

Our program will work hand-in-hand with the administration ensuring that our student-athletes represent the school with class and respect. I believe football is the front porch to your high school. It involves so many people, including members of the band, color guard, dance team, cheerleaders, fans, parents, community and so many more. If football players work with the administration, we can use the influence of football, which helps kick off the school year, as a catalyst for a great academic season, as well as a great football season. Once we identify the key cultural characteristics, we can get to work. If I see rat droppings in the gym, I don't need to see the rat, the droppings are evidence the rat is there. The same is true for culture. There always is undeniable evidence when rats exist. You just have to know your expectations in order to know what to look for. I worked in a very toxic culture once. However, no one knew it was toxic because they did not have an expectation of excellence. When you don't know what you want, you will take what you get. Administrators can help with building your program up because everything rises and falls on leadership.

9. Faculty

Teaching is the most important profession in the world. Almost every person you have ever met attended some sort of school and was taught by several teachers. As a part of the faculty, I will be at faculty meetings when I am not monitoring students. I will be in the hallways. I will poke my head in and out of classes to make sure our players are doing what is expected of them. I will not try to do the job of the classroom teacher, principal, athletic director or dean.

We will use the second home game as teacher appreciation night. We also will give teachers thank you cards and free tickets to the annual sports banquet. We want every teacher to feel like he or she is part of the team's success. The players will sit in the first two rows of the classroom, if the instructor approves. If a student is not behaving or is not on task, the teacher can text me, and I will be there immediately. We will use the influence of playing time to encourage players to behave and do things the right way.

10. Getting Students into College

Getting students into college is like making a sandwich. The student-athlete is the meat of the sandwich, the most important part. The coach is the bread, a key ingredient. Parent, teachers, community members and other supporters act as the condiments, lettuce, tomatoes, onions, etc. I believe if a high school student plays football for four years in a real program, he can play college football. The reason I didn't play at Alabama, Auburn, Florida or Florida State is because I wasn't good enough. This is the reality for 95 percent of our team members. Playing at the highest level has to do with size, speed and academics. We are not a college football factory. It is not our job to produce college football players. However, we will work hard to help each student-athlete realize his dream of playing at the next level. I have been blessed to build relationships with several college recruiters over the years. While at Jefferson County and Vernon, we set a record and signed every senior. Getting students into college is a year-round job. Camps, film, transcripts, statistics and reference letters are part of the process. Playing college football and earning a college football scholarship are two different things.

11. Strength and Conditioning

In 2016, I was the head weightlifting coach at Vernon High School, and we won the state championship. The man that made the biggest difference was acting Head Coach Lee Richards. He knew more about weighlifting than I did. Hiring people who know more than you is usually a wise decision. I have spent time at top high schools that have made tremendous gains in the weightroom, earning several state runner-up titles and state championships.

We will lift weights year-round with four goals in mind:

1. Safety
2. Prevent Injury
3. Build muscle
4. Speed, Conditioning and Flexibility

We will train very hard in the weightroom. The stronger the player, the more aggressive he will play. Players who are very strong tend to play with a lot of confidence. Our weight-training program is designed to help prevent athletic injuries and produce strong, lean and flexible players. We especially concentrate on the core and on getting the athlete faster.

The workout we will use is safe, comprehensive, proven, and very challenging. This training will show the coaches which players want to win and which players just want to be on the team. If a player cheats, quits or gives up in the weightroom, he will do the same on the field.

12. <u>Junior Varsity and Youth Teams</u>

In a perfect world we would have four youth leagues. Players would wear the same colors as the high school players, practice on the high school field, spend time with the high school players and coaches and play games on the game field. The youth league coaches would attend every day of spring football training and learn what we do and how we do it. This would produce an organic culture conducive to growth of the football program. The reason many programs don't reach their full potentials is because they neglect the younger players.

When I served as an assistant coach at Camden County High School, we were successful because of the attention to detail in our sub-varsity programs. These teams ran the same plays and used the same terminology. Imagine a young man running the same plays from third grade until he played in high school. His confidence would be unbelievable. Repetition is the mother of learning. If the head coach oversaw one of the middle school teams and one or two youth teams, it would pay great dividends. We would all use the same terminology, same drills, same practice schedule and same structure in an effort to create a winning culture. We would want those coaches at our practices and games, and I would attend their practices and games.

Repetition is the mother of learning

13. <u>Equipment</u>

Players' safety and health are top priority. We will cut back in other areas if needed to ensure that our players are protected with the safest and best-fitting equipment. I am brand loyal to Douglas and Riddell. However, we will use what is available until we can afford the best equipment.

Helmets and shoulder pads are the two most important items to upgrade, if needed. During my first 30 days on the job, we will inventory the equipment. A competent equipment manager is just as important as a good offensive or defensive coordinator. Our top 20 players must have the best equipment, but good equipment can still be a year or two old. The word "uniform" means everyone is alike, and I am big on this principle. Jerseys and pants will be worn correctly. I prefer the jersey tops that are tight-fitting (so opponents can't hold and grab our jerseys) but are shorter and don't have to be tucked in. Everyone will wear the same-colored shirt underneath their pads, and we always will be in school colors. This includes during practice, in the weightroom and during any other non-formal team function. We will wash players' uniforms after games and practices and reissue them. Part of our inventory check will include weightroom and field equipment. We must work toward getting the basics, which include a chute, dummies, balls, cones, sled, rings and tires, and some specialty equipment. It is important to have the right equipment to put players in a position to achieve success.

14. Field Maintenance

At Carver we played at an unbelievable community stadium called Cramton Bowl. I had no responsibility as far as maintaining the field turf or stadium. At Escambia and Vernon, we had a grass stadium that my staff and I maintained with help from community members and school administrators. This is a very important issue, and there has to be a plan for year-round maintenance.

15. Practice

Practice is my favorite part of coaching. I believe the hardest thing in sports is not hitting a fastball or standing in the cage of a UFC fight but to practice football four days a week, 20 weeks a year. I love football practice. We will work so hard in practice that the games will be easy. If you go watch Florida State, Oklahoma, Georgia Tech, Alabama or Georgia practice, you will get an idea of what our practices are like. I have watched these teams practice in recent years, and it is exciting. No standing around. A lot of moving parts. There is uplifting music and cheering!

I'm a livewire - like Pete Carroll was when he was at the University of Southern California. Here is an excerpt from an article on Coach Carroll: *"I think you can have a great time playing this game, coaching this game. I have a need to find fun and make it fun for the players and coaches." Carroll doesn't believe in closed practices. He allows the players' families to visit and watch from the sidelines. When the players have a pickup basketball game, Carroll is usually in the middle of it. He has been known to jump in the pile during a scrimmage wearing no padding, but laughing just the same."*

This describes me exactly. Even though I'm a player's coach, I do not lack discipline. Discipline is my strongest asset. That's why I encourage other coaches to watch us practice. God has blessed me with the ability to mix the two pretty well.

16. Summer Camps

If approved by the Principal we will go to several 7-on-7 summer tournaments, a lineman camp and a Fellowship of Christian Athletes padded camp. The goal of camps is to come closer as a team and to improve athletically.

17. Game Planning

Coaches will have Saturdays off to spend with their families. We will meet at 3 p.m. on Sundays to put a game plan together. We will first meet as a staff to talk about the previous game and the next opponent. Each coach is expected to grade the film of our previous game and the next opponent. Each coach will fill out a worksheet about the film of our opponent, and it is due at 3 p.m. Sunday, at the start of our meeting.

After the general meeting, which will include special teams, we will eat dinner together, which hopefully, the booster club can provide. After dinner, we will split up into two groups. Offense and defense will meet separately. When these meetings are finished, we all will get to work on our weekly duties. The duties include putting the scouting report together, making the bulletin board for that week, posting the players' grades for the game and cutting film for our players to watch. We will always be prepared and we will always focus on the little things.

Dean Smith wrote in his book *Leadership Lessons from a Life in Coaching*: "A steady focus on taking care of the little things, attending diligently to the many details involved with building a team. Helped us produce a mind-set that enhanced our ability to handle the big things. Handling details haphazardly often leads to treating the bigger things carelessly, and those things determine the outcome of games."

With that in mind, we will work hard during the week and Friday night will be "payday."

18. Game Day Organization

This goes back to the little things. We will be very organized. On home games the students will not be allowed to leave the facilities. We will give them an itinerary on Monday as part of their scouting report that covers our hour-by-hour schedule for the entire week. We will eat breakfast together, and the meal will be provided by the booster club or a local church. We will receive a devotional and then head to school. If there is a pep rally, we will attend and participate. After school, we will eat a pre-game meal, have meetings, athletic taping, stretching and pre-game warmups, then on to VICTORY.

Each coach will have a list of duties. If there is no stadium manager, these duties will include stadium duties for home games. The coordinators and I will have our call sheets with us to help us call plays, and we will be the only ones allowed to call timeouts. I will be the only coach allowed to talk to the referee, and we will have methods of dealing with substitutions for injuries and any other unforeseen issues. Game day is like opening night of a Christmas play or recital. We work on our parts all week, have dress rehearsals on Thursday and strive for perfection on Friday nights in front of our audience.

19. Home Games

We will try to get local churches to feed us on game days if the booster club is not able to do so. With or without the church feeding us, we will ask a local youth minister to give us words of encouragement if possible. This helps to get the community involved, and it helps the community take ownership of the team. On game day we will dress alike. This could include jerseys, matching polos, jumpsuits or T-shirts. Four times a year, we will wear ties to school on a Tuesday. The purpose of dressing up a few times a year is to make sure every player knows how to tie a tie and how to dress for success. This is one of many life skills we hope to teach throughout the year. We also teach players how to order a steak, write a check, mail a letter, prepare a resume, interview for a job and change a tire.

20. Away Games

It is important to have a detailed travel itinerary for away games. The opposing players have the advantage because they are playing in a familiar place. However, we don't have to give them an even greater advantage because we are not organized. I like to arrive at away games 90 minutes before kickoff to give our student-athletes time to relax, focus, walk the field and get dressed. Some games we arrive dressed, and some games we will not, depending on the distance and weather. Seniors and juniors will ride on the lead bus, and everyone else will ride on the second bus. Once we get there, they will have time to meet with their position coaches and review special teams.

We can still have the same plan for pre-game as we do for home games. However, we will need a post-game meal whenever we play outside the city. Usually, two double cheeseburgers and an apple pie from McDonald's and a Gatorade will work just fine. Once we are 30 minutes away from the game site, there is no talking, and if we lose the game there is no talking on the way back.

21. <u>Media and Social Media</u>

It is important to cultivate positive relationships with the media and to represent our school and football program with class. An assistant will call in scores to media outlets after the game as well as post them on our various social media outlets. I will give a quote from me to the assistant in case the media asks for one. We will role play with the players on how to talk to the media. We also will have a social media workshop about the pros and cons of social media and a social media policy in which the players will sign.

22. <u>Physicals and Other Paperwork</u>

The best way to do physicals is to get a bus and take the entire team during the summer. We will have a pot luck for all players and their families two times a year. At this event we will have a notary present to notarize required forms.

23. <u>Forever Learning</u>

I try to read a book a month. It's not difficult. Read 30 minutes in the morning, 30 minutes before you go to bed and for an hour on both Saturday and Sunday. I love improving myself as a person and a coach. I go to clinics, and I talk to other coaches. I am forever learning. A couple of years ago my staff and I visited more than 20 different places in one off-season. It

> **Applied knowledge is a key component in creating an advantageous culture**

was amazing. We learned so much. It changed our program. Applied knowledge is a key component in creating an advantageous culture.

24. <u>FOOTBALL</u>

Finding the right fit is so important. It is so much more than just football.

With that being said, what we do on offense will be based on our personnel, although our goal is to have a balanced offense. Our defense will consist of our top players. We will be an odd front with two high safeties. Our base coverage will depend on the skill set of the athletes we have. We will start with cover 4. It's' the easiest.

As a head coach, manager or person in charge, it is important that everyone knows what the leader's expectations are.

Coaching Expectations

<u>General</u>

- Be supportive of the school completely - in all sports, all activities.
- Be loyal to the football program and school.
- Present a unified front in all situations, at all times.
- Act and dress professionally in public at all times.

- Follow the chain of command if you have any problems.

School

- Be on time to all meetings and duty assignments.
- Do a great job in the classroom. A bad teacher is almost always a bad coach and a liability to the entire program.
- When it doesn't interfere with your class preparation, use your planning period for football-related activities.

Off-Season

- Unofficially meet once meetings and duty assignments are communicated.
- Monitor academic progress of all your position players.
- Meet with all your position players and help plan their academic directions.
- Work with players individually to improve areas of weaknesses.
- In the weightroom, attend all assigned weightroom days and work in the weightroom with the same expectations we have during practices.
- Seek professional development opportunities.

In-Season

- Break down films on Saturdays, and begin to prepare game plans and scouting reports. Make sure you and the coordinator are on the same page.
- Monitor academic progress of your roll call line and position players. E-mail teachers about helping with discipline problems and to get updates.
- Prepare your part of the scouting report.
- Meet at 3 p.m. on Sunday to plan practices for the week.

We use an evaluation form to evaluate our coaches and players. What gets measured gets done. We can't say we are on a diet yet never weigh ourselves.

EVALUATION FORM

Staff Member Name: _____**Date:** _____

**1 – Good   2 – Needs Improvement   3 – Unsatisfactory
4 – Not observed**

ADMINISTRATIVE RESPONSIBILITIES:

___ Cooperates with head coach regarding preseason paperwork (rosters & compliance lists) prior to first practice.

___ Assists with the issuance and collection of player equipment.

___ Cooperates with requests for information from the athletic office on time.

___ Abides by all relevant board of education and administrative policies and guidelines.

___ Attends state rules interpretation meetings.

___ Cooperates with booster club to enhance the athletes' experience as team.

___ Publicizes team and individual accomplishments to the media and school.

___ Supervises practice area and locker room when athletes are present.

___ Demonstrates care of school facilities and equipment.

___ Assists in preparation of a detailed inventory of team equipment and updates it after each season.

RELATIONSHIPS:

___ Demonstrates enthusiasm for working with high school athletes.

___ Cooperates with head coach regarding team philosophies, guidelines and player expectations.

___ Communicates effectively with athletes and parents.

___ Establishes and maintains good rapport with faculty, administration and coaching staff.

___ Promotes all school activities and encourages students to participate in a variety of activities.

___ Keeps commitments and is punctual.

___ Shows an interest in the athletes' academic experiences.

___ Supports team as well as individual accomplishments.

___ Cooperates with the athletic trainer in regards to athletes' physical well-being.

COACHING PERFORMANCE:

___ Conducts self in a professional and sportsmanlike manner at all times.

___ Uses professional language when coaching players in a public setting.

___ Teaches the fundamental philosophy, skills and knowledge essential to the sport.

___ Develops a well-organized practice schedule with specific objectives for each practice.

___ Uses personnel and strategies effectively in games.

___ Praises athletes for positive performances.

___ Offers constructive criticism for poor performances.

___ Maintains effective individual and team discipline at practice and in games.

___ Provides opportunities for all members of the team to participate, depending upon their ability and effort, while maintaining a competitive squad.

___ Team's performance reflects enthusiasm, motivation, proper fundamentals and sportsmanship.

___ Learns new strategies and trends in the sport by attending clinics and reading coaching publications.

HEAD COACH'S COMMENTS:

ASSISTANT COACH'S COMMENTS:

_____   _____

Assistant Coach's Signature   Date

_____   _____

Head Coach's Signature   Date

When we have our bi-annual workshops for coaches, I go over this information line by line. It is difficult to fire someone, but it's part of the role of a leader. I try to pair a resentment with an appreciation. Some call it the Oreo Method, which is to sandwich bad news with good news before and after. These methods work, but documentation works better. We put the two together, and we use this form to guide us through delivering bad news.

COACHING GUIDELINES

1. This old cliché is true: "They don't care how much you know, until they know how much you care. "Love students, and treat them like you would treat your own son."
2. Players will meet your expectations. Set the bar high
3. Get maximum reps; coach on the run. Don't stop and lecture.
4. Coach your players every play. They need to hear what they did right or wrong.
5. Everything is full speed. Don't let players loaf.
6. After chewing a player out, be sure to see him before he leaves and make him feel like coming back tomorrow.
7. Coach every player like he's an All-American.
8. Plan your practice. Know what you're going to work on before you go on the field.
9. Coach before you criticize.
10. What you teach, not what you know, is most important. Make sure you're using vocabulary that the players understand; or teach them your *term-aknowledgy*.
11. Be in the locker room after practice, and talk to players until they leave.
12. Don't threaten a player unless you plan to back it up.
13. Coaches never argue in front of players. Any disagreement should be handled after practice, behind closed doors. Never criticize another coach in front of players and never let a player be disloyal to a coach or teammate.
14. Understand that you are a **ROLE MODEL** for the young men on OUR team. Do not use foul language. Live your life in such a way that it will be worth emulating by the players. Don't just teach them football: **TEACH THEM LIFE**.
15. **ENTHUSIASM** is contagious. Be positive and excited about coaching here.

Chapter 8
How to Land an Interview
with an Organized Packet

According to the American Psychological Association, the divorce rate in America is close to 50 percent. If you only met half your payroll each month you would eventually lose your business. If half your students fail state standardized tests, you lose your opportunity to influence future students at the school. If your business only serves half your customers, you will go out of business. Imagine a coach going five hundred year after year. Oh, wait. That won't happen. That coach would lose his job.

A high failure rate should cause a change in the process. We date and date until we find the person we want to marry. This, though, hasn't necessarily been proven to be the best way to find a mate.

The same is true in the way we hire people. The education statistics in America are worse than the marriage and divorce statistics; however, we continue to do the same things over and over again expecting different results. We all know what that is called.

I have friends who are doctors, lawyers, bank presidents, principals, coaches and small business owners. I talked to these friends and asked them about their hiring processes. The problem with hiring head football coaches and principals starts with the process in how you go about doing it.

The committee should start with the end in mind. How can you know enough about a person in one short job interview? Knowing this is critical to you landing an interview, and focusing on these five factors will help you get into the interview chair:

1. Identify the job you want now. I identified Thomasville High School four years before I became their offensive coordinator. I identified George Washington Carver High School five years before I applied. When you identify the type of job you want it will help you with the second step.
2. Build relationships with stakeholders. The people doing the hiring usually don't know what they want. Therefore, you have to help them. You do this by planting seeds through networking and relationship building.
3. Use social media as the resume of your character and work ethic. Only post religious, political or controversial opinions if you think it will help you.
4. Build a PowerPoint version of your resume with the name and logo of the company or school you are pursuing. Everyone will send a traditional resume. How will you stand out? This vision version of your education, experiences and references may prove to be the difference-maker.
5. Find out who is on the committee. Go to their social media pages, and find out everything you can about them. Use that information to write your cover letter, prepare your hiring packet and to have certain references call them.

When I interview for head football coaching jobs I bring a binder into the interview with which most candidates cannot compete. I believe the same type of resources will impress anyone who is hiring for any profession. I have enclosed some of the information in this book. However, if you want the actual packet you will have to visit our website.

Table of Contents

COACHING DUTIES

HEAD COACH
- Offensive, defensive and kicking game plan
- Total organization and follow-up
- Student, faculty and community relations
- Prepare overall practice plan
- Prepare offensive practice plan with OC
- Prepare defensive practice plan with DC
- Prepare special teams practice plan with coordinator
- Booster Club/Parent Meeting activities
- Budget
- Facilities improvements
- Football clinics
- Player Punishment
- Scouting report
- Weekly play sheet
- Weightroom plan with Strength Coach
- Travel with DFO
- Study Hall with Academic Coordinator
- Field Maintenance with field crew
- College recruiting coordinator
- Rotating lock up which includes laundry

ASSISTANT HEAD COACH
- In charge when Head Coach is not present
- Scheduling
- Upload practice and game film
- Coordinate meals for coaches meeting
- Junior Varsity Head Coach
- In charge of emergency action plan
- Rotating lock up which includes laundry

DIRECTOR OF FOOTBALL OPERATIONS
- In charge of all eligibility and paperwork including physicals reports to HC and AD

- Travel
- Team meals
- Parent liaison
- Social media assistant
- Transcripts
- In charge of hudl
- Rotating lock up which includes laundry
- Roll Call Sheet
- Weather report

DEFENSIVE COORDINATOR
- On sideline on game day
- In charge of defense
- In charge of safeties
- Prepare defensive practice and game plan
- Opponents hash tendencies, down and distance, etc
- Defensive script
- Scout cards
- Defensive subs and calls
- Defensive scouting report
- Extra Point, Field Goal Block Unit
- Go over defensive game plan with Head Coach
- Rotating lock up which includes laundry

OFFENSIVE COORDINATOR
- In box on game day
- In charge of offense
- Offensive line coach
- Prepare offensive practice and game plan
- Opponents formation tendencies and personnel
- Offensive script
- Scout cards
- Offensive scouting report
- Offensive subs and calls
- Extra Point, Field Goal Unit
- Go over offensive game plan with Head Coach
- Rotating lock up which includes laundry

SPECIAL TEAMS COORDINATOR
- On sideline on game day
- In charge of special teams
- Special Teams scouting report
- Huddle special teams on the sideline and get call from Head Coach
- Keep track of daily goals and competition during practice
- Equipment room assistant
- Rotating lock up which includes laundry

RUNNING BACKS, KICKERS, SNAPPERS & HOLDERS
- On sideline on game day
- In charge of kickers, snappers and holders
- In charge of running backs
- In charge of scout offense huddle number two
- Scouting report submission
- Reading program coordinator
- Rotating lock up which includes laundry

EQUIPMENT MANAGER
- In charge of all equipment
- In charge of cameras and all video equipment
- In charge of headphones
- In charge of managers and water during practice
- In charge of pregame, halftime and post game setup
- In charge of managers

DEFENSIVE LINE
- On sideline on game day
- In charge defensive line
- Defensive special teams duty TBA
- Scouting report submission
- Rotating lock up which includes laundry

LINEBACKERS
- On sideline on gameday
- In charge of linebackers

- In charge of scout defense
- Defensive special teams duty TBA
- Scouting report submission
- Junior varsity defensive coordinator
- Rotating lock up which includes laundry

CORNERS
- In box on game day
- In charge of 7-on-7 snake
- Scouting report submission
- Break down passing tendencies and routes
- Defensive special teams duty TBA
- Rotating lock up which includes laundry

WIDE RECEIVERS
- In box on game day
- Bulletin Board
- Scouting report submission
- Break down defensive coverage tendencies
- Offensive special teams duty TBA
- Rotating lock up which includes laundry

STRENGTH AND CONDITIONING
- In charge of weightroom
- In charge of testing
- In charge of conditioning
- Works with trainer on injury report

ACADEMIC COORDINATOR
- In charge of study hall
- In charge of raising the bottom twenty five percent
- In charge of reward program
- NCAA workshops for parents
- Academic packets for college coaches
- Schedule academic college tours

TRAINER
- Provided by local sports medicine doctor

- In charge of injury report
- In charge of taping
- In charge of rehab
- In charge of concussion protocol

SPIRITUAL COORDINATOR
- Responsible for spiritual growth of players and coaches (if they want it)
- Give out cards on birthdays and anniversaries
- Spiritual advisor and counselor
- Hospitality committee (weddings, births, death, sickness, cards, flowers, etc.)
- Lead coaches bible study
- In charge of summer daily devotionals
- Must be present two days a week at practice and all games
- Coordinate pre game breakfast and meal with local churches

Chapter 9
Importance of the
Fellowship of Christian Athletes

The Fellowship of Christian Athletes does an excellent job of adding value to the lives of students and coaches. FCA has changed my life with its on-campus huddle, coaches' Bible studies, community outreaches and summer camps.

During my first year of coaching I had two all-state players get in some major trouble. One of them ended up serving time in prison, and the other ended up missing his senior year of football due to his poor choices. Before they got into trouble I talked to them about their grades, the weightroom and football techniques. However, I never mentioned my faith. I failed both of those young men. I realized that no matter how hard we push them in the weightroom their bodies are going to fail them one day. No matter how much they learn in school their minds will fail them one day. I believe the most important parts of their beings are their souls, and their souls will not fail them. Their souls will spend eternity in a place with air conditioning or in a place without air conditioning.

After the incident with those two players I decided to always share my faith with my players. I do not beat them over the head with it or tell them that their faith is wrong. I intentionally live a life that exemplifies my beliefs while mentioning my faith at appropriate times.

In 2003, Coach Kirk Harrell invited me to join him, his family and a few students on a trip to Black Mountain, North Carolina, for a Fellowship of Christian Athletes camp.

That second week in July changed my life. Former Duke University Head Football Coach Fred Goldsmith led our Bible study that week. He told us when he worked as an offensive coordinator he used a large laminated play call sheet to call plays. He said he now uses a similar sheet to do the most important thing a person can do. Pray.

Coach Goldsmith had organized a prayer play sheet. I adopted this way of speaking to God, and it has served me and others well. I thought about putting the actual diagram in this book, but instead I will give you the basic concept that I use. If you are a person of faith, you probably find yourself saying, "I will pray for you," when people are going through difficult times. I don't know about you, but although I have good intentions, I often forget to pray for those people. The prayer play sheet helps me remember; I put names in my phone, and I pray for them on Saturdays. I try to repent and pray a prayer of thanksgiving daily, but unfortunately, I need a reminder to pray for others. The prayer play sheet helps me focus on praying for a specific group of people by name on a weekly basis.

- Sunday - immediate family, pastors and their families, my side of the family by name, health
- Monday - my wife's side of the family by name, law enforcement, first responders, peace
- Tuesday - our children's future spouses, politicians, my administration, former players, grace
- Wednesday - coaches and their families, my coaches and their families by name, my church
- Thursday - the athletes I coach by name, armed forces and U.S. Military
- Friday - adoration, confession, thanksgiving, salutation
- Saturday - People from my "I'll pray for you" prayer list, people who are ill and new friends, the United States.

We take our players to a faith-based camp every year, and it is usually an FCA camp. This can be expensive, but to us, it is a priority. The way we raise money is by building relationships with pastors and business owners who are believers. We ask each church to sponsor one student-athlete and each business owner to do the same. When camp is over we have the players write a letter about their experience, and we send it to the churches and business owners to thank them for making it all possible. We start this process in January, and by the summer, we usually have enough money to pay for camp, or at least cut the cost in half. Several coaches have made a vow to start their fall seasons off with a team FCA camp.

Appomattox, Virginia, is a small county in the center of the state of Virginia known for its rich Civil War history. The football team there is another reason the community is gaining notoriety. In recent years, the team has won the state championship three seasons in a row. Their story is remarkable. During this three-year span, the community suffered unbelievable tragedy including death, a major storm and personal problems that impacted the team directly. Their head football coach did a tremendous job of keeping his team together. Great coaches wear several hats: coach, counselor, preacher, psychologist and teacher. He did not have a five-star athlete or players with scholarship offers from any teams in the power five conferences.

> **Great coaches wear several hats: coach, counselor, preacher, psychologist and teacher**

Doug Smith arguably has been the best football coach in the country during the past three years. He credits part of his team's success to starting each season off with the Fellowship of Christians Athletes football camp. He believes this camp reinforces their culture. It is hard to argue with a guy who has won three state championships.

I have always taken our teams to FCA Camp. I probably could write an entire book about the impact of FCA on my life. In high school and college I was an active FCA member. I have served as a huddle coach at several high schools. I actually took a season off from coaching to work for FCA full-time. Most summers I find myself speaking at different FCA Camps, along with speaking at leadership camps and to campus huddles. I absolutely love FCA. I love the magazine, the T-shirts, the Bibles, the resources and what it has meant to my family.

A few years ago my family and I were scheduled to go on a Disney cruise. We were all excited because although my wife and I had vacationed on a few different cruise ships, and I had worked on a Disney cruise line, we had never all cruised together. One day our daughter asked me if we had to go on the Disney cruise. I was puzzled, but I told her we had to go because we already paid for the trip. I asked her why she did not want to go. She said she would rather go to FCA Camp. She was under the impression that we had replaced FCA Camp with the cruise. I assured her that we would not miss FCA Camp.

When a successful coach says they tried a new offense, defense, technique or product, we want to see what it is all about. Coach Smith just won three state championships in a row, and he recommends FCA Camp. FCA Camp is powerful because it reinforces what most coaches are teaching their athletes. It really is special when your players see another team being coached the same way they are coached. The bond that is created at camp cannot be duplicated anywhere else.

I love church, but FCA Camp is not church. I love team camps, but this is so much more. The fact that the FCA staff has prayed for your players prior to them arriving at camp is special. The fact that each staff member intentionally plans activities to help your athlete maximize what God has given them is incredible. None of us knows what each season will bring. We don't know if there is going to be a death, a school shooting, a cancer diagnosis, a tropical storm, tornado or

We have no idea what the future holds, but FCA reminds us of who holds the future

hurricane. We have no idea what the future holds, but FCA reminds us of who holds the future.

I consider myself an "FCA Guy." I don't like that term, but people have called me that. I know several coaches in South Georgia who are the definition of "FCA Guys," but as I go around the country to talk to successful head coaches, many of them believe faith is an important part of what they do each day. I have found successful coaches of different sports in different states who believe the Fellowship of Christian Athletes organization is a key component to their success.

Football Coach Rick Jones from Greenwood High School in Greenwood, Arkansas, has played for 10 state championships and won seven of them. His overall coaching record is 295-72. He has been named Coach of the Year 16 times including being named National Federation of High Schools Football Coach of the Year in 2012. He is a Hall of Fame coach with more wins and awards than any high school football coach I have ever met. Coach Jones credits faith as a key component to his success as a coach.

I could name youth league FCA Guys like Joe Mahuron or middle school FCA Guys like Mike Phares or more high school FCA Guys, but you may not know who they are. So, I will name big-time college and professional coaches that could be considered FCA Guys or FCA Gals. My purpose for mentioning these coaches is to show you that FCA Camp won't make your team soft or unaggressive. FCA Camp and your local FCA campus huddle will do just the opposite. I believe it will bring your team closer together and encourage them to play harder for something bigger than themselves. You can embrace FCA and still have success in the win column.

Top FCA Coaches:

- John Wooden - While at UCLA, he won 10 national basketball championships.
- Patty Gasso - Head softball coach, University of Oklahoma, has won four national championships and is close to 1,150 wins.

- Tony Dungy - Won the Super Bowl while coaching the Indianapolis Colts.
- Bobby Bowden - While at Florida State University, his team won 377 football games and two National Championships.
- Chanda Rigby - Head Coach Troy University Women's Basketball with more than 500 career wins.
- Dabo Swinney - Currently at Clemson, where he has more than 100 wins, a national championship and several coach of the year honors
- Doug Pederson - Won Super Bowl LII as the head football coach of the Philadelphia Eagles.
- Mark Richt - Has more than 160 college football game wins at the University of Georgia and the University of Miami, a few conference championships in two of the top conferences and several coach of the year honors.
- Kay Yow - Women's basketball coach who has won more than 700 games at Elon and North Carolina State.
- Tom Osborne - Former member of the U.S. House of Representatives who has won three national football championships and more than 250 games.
- Fisher Deberry - While at Air Force, his teams won the Commander in Chief Trophy 14 times and shared it once, and he was named 1985 Football Coach of the Year by several publications.
- Sue Semrau - Head coach, Florida State University Women's Basketball, with 13 NCAA tournament appearances, the winningest coach in school history and a 4-time ACC Coach of the Year.

This is not a list of perfect humans. That list would only have one name. This is a list of coaches who have inspired me to not be ashamed of my faith. I hope you are saying, "What about this coach, and what about that coach?" That would mean you know coaches who have won at a high level that didn't hide their faith. There is a Bible verse that says when someone lights a candle, they don't put it under a bushel or a bowl, they set it out so it can light the entire house. You know the song little children sing, "This little light of mine, I'm going to let it shine."

The coaches I mentioned are a beacon for all of us to see. Music like "This Little Light of Mine" is powerful. I believe one of the great factors when creating culture is music. Music is often used in sports. I honestly believe music can change the culture of a program faster than any other resource.

The first thing we do at every program we take over is change the music in the weightroom. We find good music with a good message. It doesn't matter if the players don't like the music. They aren't in control. I am. Many young people are used to having a choice in what happens. I'm old school. We have a liaison team that represents the team's voice, but I have seen music change our team's demeanor. Therefore, I don't budge on this matter.

As an assistant coach I felt like a hypocrite several times because of the decisions we made as a staff. I did not agree with the decisions, but in public I said I did because I was a member of the staff.

At one school we suspended players for drinking at a party, but the country music we listened to in the weightroom glorifies alcohol use and abuse. At another school we suspended players for smoking weed, but the hip hop music we listened to promoted drug use and abuse. At another school we reprimanded a young man for having sex on campus, but the music we played in the stadium promoted this type of behavior. It's hypocritical.

I am not judging anyone, I just don't agree with holding someone accountable for behaviors we permit, support and promote. I have worked at two universities. At one of the institutions we suspended guys for using profanity on a rap video. The staff used profanity often, and the music was laced with profanity, yet we suspended the players for foul language.

I have found good music that promotes leadership and teamwork instead of popular music today that promotes me, myself and I. We are fighting a culture of entitlement. Young people today have only lived in a culture of I and me.

The Internet even starts with an I. So does iPhone and iPad and iMovie.

I made it my business to learn more about the generation I was teaching and coaching. Their attitude toward an uncertain future is, "I'll learn to cope." The way they communicate is short and with symbols. They want feedback instantly and on a screen. Whereas my generation wanted freedom to work on our own or not to work at all, this generation wants to do things their own way. These findings come from Dr. Tim Elmore, who says my generation used entertainment for pleasure, while this generation employs it. The most effective way to create culture is to know as much as you can about the occupants of the environment.

A few years ago I took over a program with a questionable environment. Players used profanity, smoked during film sessions and admitted to me that 90 percent of the team used marijuana on a regular basis. They were pretty upset that I wouldn't let them listen to their favorite song called "Watch Me." A teenager named James Metoudi, who called himself Silento, performed a song called "Watch Me." In the summer of 2015 it was one of the most popular songs in America. The players did not understand why we could not play the song in the weightroom. They came at me with facts and examples of why we should play it. They told me the song did not have any bad language. They mentioned that the song is played at the stadium and that their parents even like the song. They also told me that they saw my son doing the dances that go with the song.

The problem with the song is its message. The message of the song goes against everything we were trying to accomplish as a team. Plus, they proved that they listened to that song everywhere else. Therefore, it was not necessary to listen to it in the weightroom, as well. Although the song doesn't have actual verses - or what us old people would call lyrics - it does have a message. It's an innocent message, yes, but in my opinion a counter-productive message to team culture. The message of the song says, "I would rather have 2,000 yards rushing and lose every game than have 200 yards rushing and win every game."

The song uses the phrase "Watch Me" 65 times. This song does not use profanity like most popular songs of the day, but I just didn't want our players saying "Watch Me." I wanted them to say "Watch Us."

Through my research I found two things. The Health Science Academy says music has been classified a performance-enhancing drug and cannot be used in sanctioned track and field competitions. Other research suggests music has an emotional effect on the brain, and therefore, on performance. I have witnessed music affect moods and demeanors. The second thing I found in my research is that some artists who make music actually reinforce the culture we're trying to create.

These are my top 10 artist recommendations for your sports team. These are not my top 10 favorite artists, but artists who I believe will help create a winning culture in the weightroom and at practice. You will have to search each artist to find songs that have tempos you want for your weightroom and practices.

1. Derek Minor
2. NF
3. Andy Mineo
4. K.B.
5. Flame
6. Lecrae
7. Bizzle
8. Trip Lee
9. Ty Brasel/ Swoope
10. Aha Gazelle

If you want to have an amazing impact on people, combine their passions with a positive message that moves them emotionally. Sports, positive music and FCA are an equation for success.

You are creating culture whether you want to or not. Be intentional.

Eight of my former assistant football coaches have served as head coaches. Many of them used these strategies, principles and information to help them land their job. Most of them use our culture model in their program every day.

I hope the information in this book helps you realize your potential to lead your own program one day.

Made in the USA
Middletown, DE
24 October 2023

41292363R00071